Sailor's Tales

Thanks mainly to the novels of C S Forester, Patrick O'Brian and Dudley Pope, there has been a upsurge of interest in the navy and sea life in the age of sail. This new series of contemporary memoirs and autobiographies fully supports the old notion that truth is stranger that fiction, since the best of the sailors' own tales are just as entertaining, informative and amusing, while they shed faithful light on the curious and outlandish world of the seaman. Avoiding the oft-reprinted or anthologised pieces, 'Sailors' Tales' offers only the rarest and most authentic accounts; but just as impor-tantly they have been selected for their entertainment val⸳⸳ much enhanced in these newly designed editions.

NELSONIAN REMINISCENCES

Leaves from Memory's Log

---

*A Dramatic Eye-Witness Account of
the War at Sea 1795–1810*

G.S. Parsons
LIEUT. RN

*Edited with notes by
W H LONG*

Introduction by Michael Nash

CHATHAM PUBLISHING

LONDON

Publisher's Note

This edition was typeset from the 1905 edition, edited
and with notes by W H Long, except that Long's Introduction
has been replaced by a new one by Michael Nash.

Published in 1998 by
Chatham Publishing,
61 Frith Street, London W1V 5TA

Chatham Publishing is an imprint of Gerald Duckworth & Co Ltd

First published in 1843 in Boston, Mass.
Published in volume form in
1905 by Gibbings & Company, London

British Library Cataloguing in Publication Data
A catalogue record for this book is
available from the British Library

ISBN 1 86176 084 1

Introduction © Michael Nash 1998

Type format of this edition © Chatham Publishing 1998

Typeset by Inde-Dutch Systems (India) Ltd

Printed and bound in Great Britain
by The Cromwell Press, Trowbridge, Wilts

Contents

Introduction to the New Edition by Michael Nash   vii

Naples Bay in 1799   1

Capture of the *Guillaume Tell*, now called the *Malta*   15

Leaves from Memory's Log   37

The Night Attack   73

The Mad Captain   79

Blockade of the Island of Curaçoa   89

Storming of the Dutch Camp   99

Scenes in the West Indies   107

The Sea Bear   113

Tom Allen   127

Billy Culver   133

Sir Sidney Smith   137

The Battle of St Vincent   163

Appendix: Recollections of Tom Allen,
the Last of the Agamemnons   175

Index   185

Introduction

The hazards of long distant memory were graphically highlighted during a lecture given by Dr Andrew Gordon in Portsmouth in July 1997. He cited as an example the case of a young naval officer in the Falklands conflict who clearly remembered seeing the Exocet striking the *Atlantic Conveyor*—but later realised he was on the opposite side of the escort ship when the attack occurred!

Some nineteenth-century historians felt that Parsons suffered from this malady. Nelson's American biographer, Captain Mahan, wrote to John Knox Laughton on 20 March 1896: "What do you think of Parson's 'Nelsonian Reminiscences?' I think the man is telling the truth, as far as his memory serves him but you would be a better judge." Laughton in fact dismissed the book as being. "Of very doubtful value. Second-hand reminiscences of a boy of twelve or fourteen after the lapse of more than forty years are not worth much." Oman, in more recent times, was a little more realistic. "Parsons' recollections are hopelessly confused as to date, ... but he is clear as to individual incidents." Hilda Gamlin, Lady Hamilton's biographer and staunch supporter, who lived only a mile or two from Parson's final home, rallied to his defence. In 1899 she wrote: "The really reliable Reminiscences ... have been received with contemptuous remarks by recent Nelsonian writers, merely, it would seem, in order to detract from the word of one who spoke well of Emma ... from personal observation." Charles Britton, a writer who produced a useful Nelson study in 1946, would have agreed. He described Parsons' work as: "A breezy and interesting book of Nelsonian recollections—all too rare."

Laughton, as befits his calling, dealt only in hard indisputable facts, but perhaps in doing so too readily dismissed a remarkable book. The value of Parsons' work lies not in pin-point accuracy, but rather in the fascinating recollections—made no less so by the hazards of long distant memory—of a seaman who stood in the shadows and quietly witnessed the great historical events which unfolded around him. Parsons' memoirs describe the seismic scenes played out on the decks of the *Foudroyant* in the late 1790s, through to the author's retirement on half-pay in 1810.

Originally published in detached portions in the *Metropolitan Magazine* between 1837 and 1840, this work first appeared in book form when it was published in Boston, in 1843. Parsons was then employed as a Superintendent of the Mails aboard Atlantic steam packets out of Liverpool. It was first published in England later that year, and various pocket-size editions popped up in the provinces between the 1840s and the 1870s. In 1905, W H Long edited an attractive edition to which he added notes, and more importantly, an index. A facsimile edition was also published in 1973.

Rich in anecdote, Parson's book includes an account of the controversial events in the Bay of Naples in 1799, and the capture of the *Guillaume Tell* which had escaped from Nelson's clutches at the Battle of the Nile. He describes the catastrophe which befell Lord Keith's flagship *Queen Charlotte* off Leghorn in 1800. The ship caught fire and blew up with only 156 survivors from a complement of 830 men. He gives an account of the Battle of St Vincent in 1797, describes blockade duty in the West Indies, and takes the reader on a night-time cutting-out expedition off the coast of France in 1810. In addition Parsons provides rare glimpses of Nelson, Lady Hamilton, Sir Sidney Smith, Caracciolo, Jervis, Troubridge, Tom Allen, Lord Keith, and other great contemporary characters.

George Samuel Parsons was born in Lambeth, Surrey, about the year 1783. He entered the Royal Navy in July 1795 as a first class volunteer in the *Barfleur*, 98, Captain James Richard Dacres, and fought in that ship as a midshipman at St Vincent in 1797. Young Parsons removed to the *Foudroyant*, 80, as signal-midshipman under Nelson,[1] and in this ship was present at the capture of *Le Genereux*, 74, *Ville de Marseilles*, armed store ship, and *Guillaume Tell*, 84.

Parsons served under Lord Keith during the expedition to Egypt and commanded a gun-boat on Lake Mareotis, receiving a Turkish gold medal for his services. In the summer of 1801 he was

[1] O'Byrne gives the date from Parson's return as April 1798 but this is incorrect. The *Foudroyant* was not launched at Plymouth until 25 May 1798, and she did not become Nelson's flagship until June 1799.

made acting-lieutenant of the *El Carmen*, and at the close of that year came home in the ship which carried Sir Sidney Smith to England. His appointment as lieutenant was confirmed in March 1802 when he joined the *Batavia*, and in the following year he served under Captain Thomas Fremantle in the *Ganges*, 74, employed off the coasts of Ireland and Spain.

The year 1805 found Parsons carrying out the duties of first lieutenant in the sloops *Racoon* and *Elk* in the West Indies, and after further service he took part in the attack on Copenhagen in 1807 aboard the *Orion,* 74. Following a period on half-pay due to illness, he was appointed senior lieutenant of the *Valiant*, 74, in May 1809. It was from this ship that he commanded the boats during a cutting-out expedition in the Basque Roads. He took part in the capture of the French frigate *Cannoniere*, 40, laden with spoils from prizes taken in the East Indies during the previous three years. Parsons also served in the blockade of St Domingo and Curaçoa (the latter under Dacres), as well as fighting an action with eleven Spanish gun-boats. In December 1810 further ill-health obliged the author to retire from active service on half-pay, and he was not officially employed again for 31 years. In 1812 he married a Liverpool girl, Catherine Giball, and had at least eleven children.

On 1 November 1841 Lieutenant Parsons was appointed Admiralty Agent in Liverpool steam packets carrying passengers and mail across the Atlantic. In 1843, the year this book was first published, he moved into 52 Seel Street, Liverpool (the house still stands) and in July that year survived the shipwreck of the packet *Columbia* which ran aground in fog outside Boston. In September he valiantly defended Lady Hamilton's reputation in a correspondence with the editors of the *Liverpool Mercury*, and this was reprinted in some later editions of his book.

On 15 February 1850, George Parsons was made commander on the Retired List. About that time he moved over to the Cheshire side of the Mersey to live at 78 Holt Hill, Tranmere, on the outskirts of Birkenhead. Here he died of congestion of the brain at the age of 71 on 20 January 1854. His funeral took place five days later when his body crossed over salt water for the last time. He was interred in St James' Cemetery, Liverpool, where a number of other sailors who had fought with Nelson found their final berth. The impressive Anglican cathedral now stands before the plot overlooking the town Parsons had made home for so many years. His legacy is this book, sometimes rambling but never dull, a book Marryat himself would have read while editing the *Metropolitan Magazine*. Parsons steps out of the pages like a character from one of Marryat's naval yarns. If he suffers occasionally from the hazards of long distant memory, the reader will surely forgive him.

Michael Nash.
Hoylake, August 1998.

Naples Bay in 1799

Eighteen ships of the line were anchored in battle order, in this beautiful bay, on the morning of the 29th of June, under the justly celebrated Nelson, whose flag floated gaily from the mizzen-top-gallant mast of the *Foudroyant*, on whose quarter-deck were seated the gallant hero of the Nile and of a hundred other victories; and, by his side, the Cleopatra of the age, the fascinating and beauteous Emma, Lady Hamilton; when a Neapolitan boat, guarded by ragged ruffians (twenty thousand of whom, led on by Cardinal Ruffo, had long been the terror of this devoted city), brought on board the Prince Caraccioli,[1] admiral of the Neapolitan fleet, and some other nobles of that land, whose place of retreat, a cave among the mountains of Calabria, had been discovered by the banditti, who now came, with these wretched men, to claim the price of their blood. The veteran admiral, who was placed under my charge, being then signal-mate to Lord Nelson, was brought on the poop strongly guarded by marines. He was a short, thick-set man, of apparent strength, but haggard with misery and want; his clothing in wretched condition, but his countenance denoting stern resolution to endure that misery like a man. He spoke a short sentence to me in pure English, as if perfectly master of the language, and was shortly ushered into our wardroom, where a court was assembled of his own officers, Count Thurn[2] sitting as president. His defence, which was spoken in a deep, manly tone, will best explain the nature of the charge.

'I am accused,' said the Prince, 'of deserting my king in distress, and leaguing with his enemies. The accusation is so far false, that the king deserted me and all his faithful subjects. It is

[1] Caraccioli was of an ancient family, and son of Prince Caraccioli, Viceroy of Sicily.

[2] Count Thurn and five senior officers of the Sicilian Navy formed the Court. The Count was a German by birth, who had entered the Sicilian service, and risen to the rank of Commodore.

well known to you, gentlemen, that our frontier was covered by an army under General Mack, superior to the advancing enemy, and you are aware that the sinews of war is money. The king collected everything that could be converted into specie, on pretence of paying that army, embarked it in his Britannic Majesty's ship *Vanguard*, even to the enormous amount of five hundred casks, and fled with it to Palermo, there to riot in luxurious safety. Who was then the traitor – the king or myself? After such uncalled for, and, I must say, cowardly desertion by the sovereign, Mack's army disbanded, for want of pay, and the French army occupied Naples. It is known to you, gentlemen, that my patrimonial possessions lay in the city, and that my family is large. If I had not succumbed to the ruling power, my children – (here his emotion was shown by the altered tone, the quiver of the lip, and the suffusion of the eyes: he quickly conquered his emotion, and continued, in the same stern tone) – would have been vagabonds in the land of their fathers. Gentlemen, some of you are parents, and I appeal to your feelings; let each of you place yourselves in my situation, and say how you would have acted; but I think my destruction is pre-determined, and this court anything but a court of justice. If I am right, my blood be upon your head, and on those of your children!'

The veteran spread his hands abroad, and presented a fine picture of a brave man in extreme peril. The court was cleared, and a very short time elapsed before it was again opened to pronounce sentence on this devoted noble. Count Thurn covered his head, and addressed the wretched old man –

'Admiral Prince Caraccioli, you have been unanimously found guilty of the charges brought against you; you have repaid the high rank and honours conferred on you by a mild and confiding sovereign, with the blackest ingratitude. The sentence of the court is, that you shall be hanged by the neck at the yard-arm of your own flagship, in two hours from this time, and may God have mercy on your soul!'

The countenance of the veteran admiral betrayed no other emotion than a stern composure.

'Hereafter,' said he, 'when you shall be called to your great account, you will weep for this unjust sentence in tears of blood. I take shame to myself in asking any favour from such men; but, if possible, I wish to be shot, as becomes my rank, and not hung up like a felon and a dog.'

'It is inadmissible,' said Count Thurn; 'and the court is hereby dissolved.'

At two o'clock in the afternoon, the veteran, with a firm step, walked into Lord Nelson's barge, and with a party of thirty of our seamen, under one of our lieutenants, was taken to his flagship, the gun fired, and the brave old man launched into eternity at the expiration of the two hours from the time the sentence had passed. The seamen of our fleet, who clustered on the rigging like bees, consoled themselves that it was only an Italian prince, and the admiral of Naples, that was hanging – a person of very light estimation compared with the lowest man in a British ship. His Majesty of Naples, the Prime Minister, Sir John Acton, and many of the foreign ambassadors, joined and took up their quarters in the *Foudroyant* two days after the execution; and my Lord Nelson removed to the first lieutenant's cabin as his sleeping apartment, giving his cabin to the king's use, and the larboard side of the main-deck for his cooks, who condescended to officiate as ours; and never did midshipmen fare so sumptuously as during the king's long stay on board the *Foudroyant*. The day was passed in administering justice (Italian fashion) to the wretches who fell into the grasp of Cardinal Ruffo's lambs, enlivened by the bombardment of St. Elmo, which we were battering in breach. At noon, dinner was served to the royal party and their guests on the quarter-deck; Lady Hamilton's graceful form bending over her harp, and her heavenly music gave a gusto to the dessert. As the sun went down, the opera singers, in a large decked galley, came alongside, and all that could delight the ear or please the eye was there to fascinate and charm.

Some days after the execution, when the name of Admiral Caraccioli had ceased to be remembered among the great and noble of the land, I was roused from my slumbers with an account of the king being on deck. Wondering at his bad taste for early rising, I hurried up, and found his majesty gazing with intense anxiety on some distant object. At once he turned pale, and, letting his spyglass fall on deck, uttered an exclamation of horror. My eyes instinctively turned in the same direction, and under our larboard quarter, with his face full upon us, much swollen and discoloured by the water, and his orbs of sight started from their sockets by strangulation, floated the ill-fated prince. All the superstition of the Italian school was called into play by this extraordinary (and, in truth, it was a fearful) apparition. The old man's grey hair streamed in the light breeze that rippled the placid waters of this lovely bay; the king and court were alarmed, and looked very pale; the priesthood, who were numerous on board, were summoned; when one, more adroit than his brethren, told the king that the spirit of his unfortunate admiral could not rest without his forgiveness, which he had risen to implore. This was freely accorded; and on Lord Nelson (who was suffering from ill health) being awaked from his uneasy slumbers by the agitation of the court, he ordered a boat to be sent from the ship to tow the corpse on shore. This unlooked for appearance of the dead did not lessen our appetite for the good things in the king's larder, or our zest for the evening's opera.

Things moved on in the same gay strain, though many hearts were breaking with incurable sorrow, and many a brilliant eye was dimmed by incessant weeping; while famine, with its attendant miseries, reigned in the populous city of Naples, preyed on by twenty thousand banditti under the primate Cardinal Ruffo, and who (I suppose in derision) were denominated the Christian army. These scoundrels, unchecked by law or justice, with no force to restrain them, freely indulged their licentious habits, and, with tiger-like ferocity, waded deep in blood. Many, very many, of Italy's beauteous daughters, and those of high rank, have I seen prostrate on our deck, imploring protection from these bloody ruffians, by whom their natural protectors had been murdered. In my mind's eye I see them now! Their graceful forms bent with misery – their dark eyes and clasped hands raised to the Father of all for mercy – their clear, olive complexion changing to a sickly hue from anguish of mind. How could men, possessing human hearts, refrain from flying to their relief? Yet, I am sorry to say, they were placed (without regard to their feelings) in polaccos, under the guidance of young English midshipmen, there to let their afflicted hearts break at leisure. Dear, amiable, and gentle sex! How infinitely greater appears to me thy share of the curse brought upon the descendants of Adam and Eve, by their disobedience, than ours! I grieve to say, that wonderful, talented, and graceful beauty, Emma Lady Hamilton, did not sympathise in the manner expected from her generous and noble nature. This lady's talents and virtues were manifold; her vices proceeded from unfavourable circumstances, to which, in some degree, we are all victims. This noble, but unfortunate lady, has been most grossly calumniated. She served the country, with unwearied zeal and activity, and in a greater degree than any female ever before had the power. She was the cause of saving millions of British property from the grasp of the Spanish king in 1797; she enabled Lord Nelson to fight the battle of Aboukir, and kept steady to our interest the fickle and dissolute court of Naples, from her influence over the daughter of Maria Theresa, then queen of that place. Her generosity and good nature were unbounded – her talents and spirit unequalled; and, to my knowledge, her heart was of softer materials than to rejoice in the sufferings of the enemies of the court, to whom both she and Lord Nelson were bound by the strongest ties of gratitude and affection. To that high sense of gratitude for benefits conferred on them must we attribute the execution of Prince Caraccioli, and some other acts much to be lamented. But poor human nature is very fallible; they sinned, and deeply sinned, through their affection to their benefactors.[3] One short tale, and I consign this unjustly treated and wonderful woman to oblivion.

On the peace of Amiens taking place, I was paid off from the frigate *Batavia*, to which I had been appointed lieutenant by Lord Keith, and served as such during the Egyptian expedition (of which more anon), and retired, from full pay to nothing and find myself, with the comfortable assurance, from those in power, that the peace promotion had taken place, and there was no hope for me. As a last resource and 'forlorn hope,' I went to Lord Nelson's seat, at Merton, and fortunately gained admission to his lordship, through his well-known and favourite servant, Tom Allen,[4] who approached his study door under some apprehension of the nature of our reception. The voice of Lord Nelson, denoting vexation, reprimanded my friend, and declared, most truly, that he was

[3] Subsequent to that execution, Lady Hamilton, with his lordship (conspicuous from the star-like decorations that occasioned his death), were skirting the sea-board of Naples, when a shot from the Castle St. Elmo disarranged the glossy curls of the beautiful Emma. 'On *board!*' said the hero and genius of *Victory*. 'Not so, my dear lord,' said her ladyship. 'Let it never be said that Nelson and Bronté was turned by a Frenchman's ball.'

[4] See Appendix.

pestered to death by young gentlemen, his former shipmates. Tom pushed me into the room, and went in search of an able auxiliary, who entered the study, in the most pleasing shape – that of a lovely and graceful woman; and, with her usual fascinating and playful manner, declared, 'His lordship must serve me.' His countenance, which, until now, had been a thunder-cloud, brightened; and Lady Hamilton was the sun that lightened our hemisphere. She, with that ready wit possessed by the fair sex alone, set aside his scruples of asking a favour of the first Admiralty Lord, by dictating a strong certificate, which, under her direction, he wrote.

'Now, my young friend,' said her ladyship, with that irresistible smile which gave such expression of sweetness to her lovely countenance, 'obey my directions minutely; send this to Lord St. Vincent, at Brentwood, so as to reach him on Sunday morning.'

My commission, as an officer, was dated the same as the aforesaid certificate. May it be made up to thee in another and a better world, sweet lady! for man's injustice in this – *where thou hast been most foully calumniated* – and thy sins and weaknesses attributed to their proper source: thy low birth and association of thy infant years, joined to the most extraordinary talent and beauty that ever adorned thy sex. Had that well-proportioned head been encircled by a diadem, thy memory would have been held up for the adoration, instead of the execration, of mankind.

The following interesting account of Lady Hamilton and Lord Nelson is extracted from *The Remains of the late Mrs. Richard Trench* (Mother of Dean Trench), published in 1862:–

'Dined at Mr. Elliot's with only the Nelson party. It is plain that Lord Nelson thinks of nothing but Lady Hamilton, who is totally occupied by the same object. She is bold, forward, coarse, assuming, and vain. Her figure is colossal, but, excepting her feet, which are hideous, well-shaped. Her bones are large, and she is exceedingly *embonpoint*. She resembles the bust of Ariadne; the shape of all her features is fine, as is the form of her head, and particularly her ears; her teeth are a little irregular, but tolerably white; her eyes light blue, with a brown spot in one, which, though a defect, takes nothing away from her beauty or expression. Her eyebrows and hair are dark, and her complexion coarse. Her expression is strongly marked, variable, and interesting; her movements in common life ungraceful; her voice loud yet not disagreeable. Lord Nelson is a little man, without any dignity.

'Lady Hamilton takes possession of him, and he is a willing captive, the most submissive and devoted I have seen. Sir William is old, infirm, all admiration of his wife, and never spoke to-day but to applaud her.

'Miss Cornelia Knight seems the decided flatterer of the two, and never opens her mouth but to show forth their praise; and Mrs. Cadogan, Lady Hamilton's mother, is – what one might expect. After dinner we had several songs in honour of Lord Nelson, written by Miss Knight, and sung by Lady Hamilton.

'She puffs the incense full in his face; but he receives it with pleasure, and snuffs it up very cordially. The songs all ended in the sailor's way, with "Hip, hip, hip, hurra," and a bumper with the last drop on the nail, a ceremony I had never heard of or seen before.'

'Went by Lady Hamilton's invitation to see Lord Nelson dressed for Court. On his hat he wore the large diamond feather, or ensign of sovereignty, given him by the Grand Seignior; on his breast the Order of the Bath, the Order he received as Duke of Bronté, the diamond star, including the sun or crescent given him by the Grand Seignior, three gold medals obtained by three different victories, and a beautiful present from the King of Naples. On one side is his Majesty's picture, richly set and surrounded with laurels which spring from two united anchors at bottom, and support the Neapolitan crown at top; on the other is the Queen's cypher, which turns so as to appear within the same laurels, and is formed of diamonds on green enamel. In short, Lord Nelson was a perfect constellation of stars and Orders.'

THE CHASE
February 18, 1800

'Deck, there! the stranger is evidently a man-of-war – she is a line-of-battle-ship, my lord, and going large on the starboard tack.'

'Ah! an enemy, Mr. Staines. I pray God it may be *Le Généreux*. The signal for a general chase, Sir Ed'ard[5] (the Nelsonian pronunciation of Edward), make the *Foudroyant* fly!'

---

[5] Captain Sir Edward Berry.

Thus spoke the heroic Nelson; and every exertion that emulation could inspire was used to crowd the squadron with canvas, the *Northumberland* taking the lead, with the flagship close on her quarter.

'This will not do, Sir Ed'ard; it is certainly *Le Généreux*,[6] and to my flagship she can alone surrender. Sir Ed'ard, we must and shall beat the *Northumberland*.'

'I will do the utmost, my lord; get the engine to work on the sails – hang butts of water to the stays – pipe the hammocks down, and each man place shot in them – slack the stays, knock up the wedges, and give the masts play – start off the water, Mr. James, and pump the ship. The *Foudroyant* is drawing ahead, and at last takes the lead in the chase. The admiral is working his fin (the stump of his right arm), do not cross his hawse, I advise you.'

The advice was good, for at that moment Nelson opened furiously on the quarter-master at the conn. 'I'll knock you off your perch, you rascal, if you are so inattentive. Sir Ed'ard, send your best quarter-master to the weather-wheel.'

'A strange sail ahead of the chase!' called the lookout man.

'Youngster, to the masthead. What! going without your glass, and be d—d to you? Let me know what she is immediately.'

'A sloop of war, or frigate, my lord,' shouted the young signal-midshipman.

'Demand her number.'

'The *Success*, my lord.'

'Captain Peard; signal to cut off the flying enemy – great odds, though – thirty-two small guns to eighty large ones.'

'The *Success* has hove-to athwart-hawse of the *Généreux*, and is firing her larboard broadside. The Frenchman has hoisted his tricolour, with a rear-admiral's flag.'

'Bravo – *Success, at her again!*'

'She has wore round, my lord, and firing her starboard broadside. It has winged her, my lord – her flying kites are flying away altogether. The enemy is close on the *Success*, who must receive her tremendous broadside.' The *Généreux* opens her fire on her little enemy, and every person stands aghast, afraid of the consequences.

[6] The *Généreux* 74, one of the ships that escaped at the battle of the Nile.

'The smoke clears away, and there is the *Success*, crippled, it is true, but bull-dog like, bearing up after the enemy.'

'The signal for the *Success* to discontinue the action, and come under my stern,' said Lord Nelson; 'she has done well, for her size. Try a shot from the lowerdeck at her, Sir Ed'ard.'

'It goes over her.'

'Beat to quarters, and fire coolly and deliberately at her masts and yards.'

Le Généreux at this moment opened her fire on us; and, as a shot passed through the mizzen stay-sail, Lord Nelson, patting one of the youngsters on the head, asked him jocularly how he relished the music; and observing something like alarm depicted on his countenance, consoled him with the information, that Charles XII ran away from the first shot he heard, though afterwards he was called 'The Great,' and deservedly, from his bravery. 'I, therefore,' said Lord Nelson, 'hope much from you in future.'

Here the *Northumberland* opened her fire, and down came the tri-coloured ensign, amidst the thunder of our united cannon.

'The signal to discontinue the firing.' And Sir Edward Berry boarded the prize. Very shortly he returned with Rear-Admiral Perrée's[7] sword, who, he stated, was then dying on his quarter-deck, with the loss of both legs, shot off by the raking broadsides of the little *Success*. This unfortunate Frenchman was under the imputation of having broken his parole, and was considered lucky in having redeemed his honour by dying in battle.

THE BALL

Lord Nelson was truly elated by capturing one of the two ships that alone made their escape from the battle of Aboukir. Leaving the squadron under Captain Ball to blockade Malta, the *Foudroyant* bore up for Palermo – there to receive the incense of refined Italian flattery, incessant balls and feedings, the smiles of beauty, and the witchery of music. The pencil of Hogarth would have been well employed in sketching our cockpit, preparing for one of these exhibitions.

'Two *dirty* shirts nearly new, for one *clean* one!' shouts a midshipman. 'Who will lend a pair of uniform breeches? for mine are worn

[7] Rear-Admiral Perrée had been captured with the frigates under his command, in June 1799, by a division of the fleet under Lord Keith.

out by pipe-clay and cleaning,' cries a second reefer. 'John, yours will fit, and you are not on turn for going. Do – there's a good fellow!'

'Excuse me, Jack, for you ruined my number one coat at your last turn-out, by rolling in the gutter, when you received that ugly cut of the stiletto from the cut-throat Italian who calls himself a marquis.'

'Ay, ay; but I am to give you one for it, made by Stultz, should we both reach old England.'

How different to this capering, fiddling, frivolous people!

When assembled on the Prado, at Palermo, to the number of fifteen, a collection was ordered by our leader to pay for the requisite carriages to the king's palace, at Colli, the splendid scene of the night's festivities. To our great dismay, each of our party had forgotten his purse, from long disuse, except one, who, after long and laborious search, produced a paulo, value fivepence. To walk four miles would not do in dancing-pumps, and to return, when in ballroom order, which had cost us a world of trouble, and tried our resources to the utmost pitch of human ingenuity – for I (the author) substituted the leg of a stocking that had once been white, for a cambric pocket-handkerchief; and most serviceable it proved; for, on crowning the statue of Lord Nelson, erected in the illuminated gardens, to the appropriate tune of Rule Britannia, which was done by his present Majesty of Naples, then a little boy, my lord's feelings were so over-come as to betray him into womanly weakness, and his trusty aides-de-camp could do no less than apply their handkerchiefs, though, in some, from a contrary feeling of mirth.

At this time, the aforesaid stocking was invaluable. But to return to our dilemma, of how we could get to Colli. The leader proposed seizing the first carriage, which he called, putting it into requisition for his majesty's service – viz., *to convey his midshipmen.* A nobleman's splendid vehicle that was standing at his palace door for the purpose of conveying the family to the royal ball, was the first that we encountered, and after a little scuffle in displacing the coachman and footman, we succeeded in lining it, inside and out, with young English midshipmen in training for future Nelsons. This notable exploit created much amazement, and, from their exclamations, displeasure in the minds of our Italian allies, and the upset of another coach, from the careless driving of our leader. This unfortunate occurrence damped our buoyant spirits, from a young and beautiful duchess having sustained considerable injury from the concussion. But beyond all description was the fairy scene presented by the illuminated palace and the gardens, the assembled royal family, the great in rank, the bold in arms, with Italy's nut-brown daughters, their lustrous black eyes and raven tresses, their elegant and voluptuous forms gliding through the mazy dance; and the whole presided over by the genius of taste, whose attitudes were never equalled, and with a suavity of manner, and a generous openness of mind and heart, where selfishness, with all its unamiable concomitants, pride, envy, and jealousy, would never dwell – I mean Emma, Lady Hamilton. These agreeables soon drove from our youthful minds all unpleasant impressions, and the kind manner in which the presiding genius attended to our wants and covered our blunders – for, for one of our young companions (now a commodore) she won at *rouge et noir* five pounds in as many minutes – most probably divining the low state of our finances; and this enabled us to retreat as gentlemen, when our entrée had been the reverse. At midnight, we were marshalled by the officers of the palace into the illuminated gardens. Gentle reader, if you have seen Vauxhall on a gala night, you may form some conception of the fairy scene, heightened by the attendance of a Turkish admiral and his officers, whose squadron lay in the bay of Palermo. Their rich and unique attire, the contemptuous gravity with which they viewed the dancing, and the attention and adoration paid to the fairest and likewise the best part of God's beautiful creation, excited in their minds astonishment, and probably disgust. Their warlike sash, studded with loaded pistols, caused terror among the fair, and acted as a repelling power, by keeping the gentle sex at a gazing distance. These grim-looking gentlemen, on making an awkward attempt to take the same liberties with the natives they saw practised with impunity by their modest allies (the diffident English), were haughtily repelled, and many a turbaned head was laid low by that handy little instrument, the stiletto. Their indignant admiral demanded the murderers, for the pleasure of impaling them; but Lord Nelson checked his fury, by anchoring the *Foudroyant* between them and the town in battle order, with an intimation that the first shot fired at our allies would be construed into a declaration of war against the Sons of the Ocean, and be resented by the

Duke of Thunder in the true Nelsonian style. An herculean-made Maltese slave, having got the shackle off one leg, jumped into the sea, and, with astonishing exertion, swam on board us with a great weight of chain attached to his right leg; never shall I forget the poor fellow's wild and earnest supplication to Lord Nelson and Lady Hamilton for protection. It drew tears from the eyes of the fair Emma, and fruitless wishes; for his lordship would not risk a war and have his flag-ship destroyed for a wretched slave. With some other youngsters interested for the poor man, I went on board the frigate he had jumped from, but our questions respecting his fate were deemed intrusive and impertinent. Great coolness for some time existed between the followers of our blessed Saviour and the impostor Mahomet. But to return to the palace gardens – the fireworks were astonishing, by their ingenuity and brilliant effect, the vast company that were moving to the centre to view a temple erected to the goddess of Fame, who, perched on the dome, was blowing her trumpet; under the portico was seen an admirable statue of our gallant hero, supported by Lady Hamilton on his right, and Sir William on his left. These statues were imposing and excellent likenesses. As we approached, the king's band played 'Rule Britannia.' At once silence prevailed. His present Majesty of Naples (then Prince Leopold) mounted the steps behind the large statue of Nelson, on which he placed a crown of laurel, richly inlaid with diamonds. The trumpets then blew a point of war, and the bands struck up with great animation, 'See the conquering hero comes!' Lord Nelson's feelings were greatly touched, and big tears coursed each other down his weather-beaten cheeks, as on one knee he received the young prince in his only arm, who, with inimitable grace had embraced him, calling him the guardian angel of his papa and his dominions. All who were susceptible of the finer feelings, showed them by their emotion; and many a countenance, that had looked with unconcern on the battle and the breeze, now turned aside, ashamed of their womanly weakness. This was the time my substitute stocking rendered great service; for I do not hesitate to say, that I sobbed as if my schoolmaster had just applied his most forcible arguments.

The king, queen, and three fair princesses, one of them beautiful, approached the trio, and warmly congratulated his lordship on the recent capture of *Le Généreux*. Dancing recommenced, and I made some awkward attempts, as partner to the youngest Princess of Castlecicallo, who good-naturedly endeavoured to get me through the Saltarella, but I fancied was glad when she exchanged me for the Prince of Palermo, whose form resembled a wasp (being pinched in the waist by his military sash), and spun round like a teetotum on the light fantastic toe, and by the elegance of his waltzing soon effaced the recollection of a clumsy English boy, whose healthy apple cheeks were his only recommendation. This splendid entertainment was concluded by some of the wildest of our youngsters attempting to break through his Majesty's foot guards, who refused to give way to their orders. They were instantly charged by the midshipmen with their dress dirks, and broken. One of the savages fired, and shot a fine boy through the thigh, who did well. For this notable and ill-timed feat, Lord Nelson stopped our leave for six months; and many an anathema was showered on us by our equally unfortunate contemporaries of the squadron.[8]

[8] This grand fête was given 3rd September 1799, the anniversary of the day on which the news of Nelson's victory of the Nile had reached Naples. The entertainment began with a magnificent exhibition of fireworks representing the battle at Aboukir and the blowing up of L'Orient. In the illuminated gardens were erected pavilions for the English, Portuguese, Russians, and Turks, over each of which were displayed the flags of the several nations in alliance with the Two Sicilies.

Capture of the *Guillaume Tell*, Now Called the *Malta*

THE BATTLE

The shattered person of Lord Nelson – for in battle he had lost an arm and an eye, and got a fractured skull – acting upon a delicate and diminutive frame (for, as Sir William Hamilton, the ambassador, justly observed, he had a great soul enshrined in a small casket), disabled and rendered him unfit for sea; therefore his flagship, the *Foudroyant*, sailed for Malta under his captain, who was *not* Sir Thomas Hardy. On arriving off Valetta, the capital of that island, a message from Commodore Sir Manly Dixon (then commanding the *Lion*, 64) was delivered through the trumpet of the commander of the *Minorca*, that he had certain intelligence, the *Guillaume Tell* would try an escape to Toulon, as she was destitute of provisions. The commodore ordered us to anchor close in with the harbour's mouth, and watch her motions. Our station was accordingly taken just out of gunshot. At midnight (the darkness being intense) a movement was observed on shore, sky-rockets exploded, and blue lights and false fires gave intimation that the *Guillaume Tell*, Rear-Admiral Decrés, was attempting an escape through our blockading squadron. The ship was put in battle order, and the crew impatiently waited the order of our captain, who, deficient in general knowledge of the French language, had acquired a phrase that, from its rarity, was deeply impressed on his mind, and influenced his conduct. He said the French were practising a *ruse de guerre*, and remaining fast at anchor. The frequent flashes and roar of heavy artillery caused a disposition in the minds of our officers to doubt the correctness of their gallant commander's judgement; and a message delivered from the *Minorca*, that the commodore had sent him to say that the *Guillaume Tell* was going large on the starboard tack, closely followed and fired into by the *Penelope* frigate; and that we, being the only ship in the squadron able to cope with such a monster, were ordered to bring her to close action instanter.

The *ruse de guerre* haunting the mind of our captain, prevented immediate obedience; and the late Sir Thomas Staines (then third lieutenant, and commanding the lower deck guns) indignantly offered to pull into the harbour of Valetta, and ascertain to a certainty whether the *Guillaume Tell*, or some substitute, was misleading the British squadron. 'I will not risk so valuable a life as yours, Mr. Staines,'[1] and things remained in the same state of quietude until broken by a shot from the *Port Mahon* brig athwart our stern, and 'Oh! the *Foudroyant*, ahoy!' from a hoarse, powerful voice, compelled the attention of our chief. 'I am ordered by Commodore Manly Dixon to express his great surprise at the inactivity of the flagship of Lord Nelson. It is his most positive orders that the *Foudroyant* cut from her anchor, and bring the *Guillaume Tell* to close action, without losing a moment's time. Nor am I to leave you, sir, until all your sails are set in pursuit of the flying enemy, with whom Captain Blackwood is in close and interesting conversation.' This gentle intimation dispersed the ideas engendered by the *ruse de guerre*, and the *Foudroyant* was crowded with all sail that could bring her into the conference of Captain Blackwood and Admiral Decrés. Our gallant ship (like the noble greyhound slipped from his leash) bounded after the flying foe at the rate of eleven knots.

I must here observe, that we had on board a Sicilian general, the Prince of Palermo, with two hundred picked men, going to reinforce and take the command of the troops besieging Malta. Now, fair and gentle reader! do not picture to your mind an old man worn out in hard service, solacing himself with an immoderate quantity of snuff dirtily taken; but present to your mind's eye the figure of Apollo Belvedere, tightly girded round the waist, and with a face that your brilliant eyes would bestow a second glance on, and you have a faint image of this veteran general of thirty, the most illustrious the Prince of Palermo, who declared, on his sacred honour, that his grand desire was to see the English fight at sea. 'They are one great people,' said his highness; and leave was granted by our chief to his 'grand desire.' This proved fortunate; for most of our marines were before Malta, and we were short-handed.

As day broke, we observed the *Lion*, with her sixty-four small guns, receiving the smashing broadside of the huge foe. It was a

[1] He died Captain Sir Thomas Staines, K.C.B.

settler, and the *Lion* retired to digest the dose. The *Penelope*, commanded by the Honourable Captain Blackwood, hung close on her stern, and the effect of his well-directed fire was seen by the dismantled state of the enemy, who now wore to receive us, and, like a gallant stag brought to bay, showed a noble front to his assailants. Here, again, our noble captain's imaginative turn hoodwinked his judgement. 'Youngster,' said he to me, 'tell the officers of the main and lower decks to remain prepared, but not to fire without my orders, as I think the *Guillaume Tell* has struck at the sight of us.' Little did he know of her chief, the valiant Decrés (afterwards Minister of Marine to Napoleon Bonaparte), nor did he calculate that this news at the batteries would throw the crew off their guard. This erroneous idea was stoutly combated by the first lieutenant and master, who judiciously observed, 'that no British man-of-war would fire into an enemy that had surrendered.'

And 'Old Soundings,' who, from the peculiar conformation of his nose, was better known among the midshipmen as 'Rigdum Funnidos,' now determined to correct his commander, and began in his own strange way of prefacing everything with 'I am thinking – I am saying,' at the same time using his right hand, as if taking bearings (from which he also attained the name of 'Chop the binnacle'), now addressed the captain as follows – 'I am thinking – I am saying, Sir Ed'ard; that is, I am thinking you had better reduce sail to working order, pass athwart her bows to windward, and then under her stern, and whether she has struck or not, it will place us in a very advantageous position; that is, I am thinking so – I am saying so, Sir Ed'ard.'

During this admirable speech, 'Chop the binnacle's' hand was moving in its usual way. Sir Edward threw as much scorn into his countenance as it was capable of expressing, and, with great hauteur, answered thus – 'Whether the enemy has struck or not, I feel certain that no person but yourself is afraid of her broadside.'

'Chop the binnacle' stood aghast, his hand worked in the usual manner, and at last out came thinking and saying, 'That he was thinking Sir Ed'ard was calling him a coward – that he would find his courage equal to his, Sir Ed'ard's – that he was at his post to obey his orders, but no more advice would he offer'; and then took his station at the conn, in a very sulky mood.

During this time the valiant Decrés was silently preparing a
settling dose of three round shot in each of his enormous guns for
us, sustaining with great patience the teasing fire of our small craft.
We are now opening her, and perceive the tri-coloured flag fluttering from the wreck of her mizen-topmast, to which it was
apparently nailed. 'Shorten sail,' said our chief, 'and back the main-
topsail'; and, jumping on a gun, he hailed the French admiral, who
(decorated in all his orders, even to the cross of the Legion of
Honour) stood conspicuously on the poop, with his sabre naked in
his hand, and a brace of pistols in his belt. 'Strike your French
colours!' bellowed our captain through his trumpet, in what he
must have thought impressive terms. The Frenchman silently and
gracefully waved his sabre – his small-arm men poured in a volley
– their tremendous artillery vomited forth their three round shot,
the concussion heeling us two streaks – the crashing of masts and
yards, with shrieks and death groans, attested well the precision of
their aim; and the destructive effect of their broadside, so closely
delivered, that our studding-sail booms were carried away against
his mainyard. *I had done good service* in the battle of St. Vincent, in
the year '97; that is, I selected, tasted, and conveyed such oranges as
I did not approve for my own eating, to Vice-Admiral Waldegrave,
and his captain, James R. Dacres, Esq., but not, through the whole
of that glorious and unprecedented victory, did I hear such a fatal
broadside as was poured into the *Foudroyant* by the *Guillaume Tell*;
it resembled a volcanic eruption, crashing, tearing, and splintering
everything in its destructive course. 'Hard up,' said our chief, 'set
the jib, and sheet home the fore-top-gallant sail' (for we had shot
past the enemy like a flash of lightning). 'The jib-boom is gone, and
the fore-topmast is badly wounded,' roared the forecastle officer;
'look out for the topmast – stand from under!' Down it came on the
larboard gangway, crushing some to pieces under its enormous
weight. Still the force of the helm, acting on the flying rate at which
we had attacked our enemy to leeward (for our captain most
magnanimously disdained to take any advantage of her crippled
state), brought his majesty's ship in contact with the leviathan foe;
and a deafening roar of artillery again rent the sky. The
Frenchman, who had twelve hundred men, had crowded his decks,
lower yards, and rigging, ready for boarding. The naked sabre
hanging by its becket from the wrist, the pistols in the belt, and the

determined look of these half-starved ruffians, quite dazzled my vision; but still it took in their valiant admiral, standing in the most conspicuous situation, and animating his men both by voice and gestures. None who beheld the anxiety of our small-arm men to shoot him, and his miraculous preservation, could doubt a special providence. His men fell around him like corn before the reaper; but there he stood in the glittering insignia of his rank, upright and uninjured. I saw a marine, who taught us the broadsword and to fire at a mark, take dead aim at the admiral within half pistol-shot; just as his finger reached the trigger, one of their forty-two pounders carried off the head, musket, and arm of this excellent marksman. Another marine (a rare instance in the corps) disgraced it by lying on the deck, and was thought wounded by my brother signal-midshipman, Mr. West, who approached with the view of rendering assistance; but when he found it rank cowardice, he obliged the man to rise, under fear of immediate death. The poor wretch had scarcely assumed the perpendicular, when a bar, that connects grape-shot, passed through both thigh bones close up to the hips, and could not be extracted. His torture lasted two days, when death relieved his sufferings.

As a contrast to the *solitary* instance of cowardice in a private marine, I must here mention the daring gallantry of one Scott, a signalman in my own department. The enemy, as usual, fired to dismast us, and the principal slaughter-house was the poop, where this slender, ruddy-complexioned youth of twenty was quartered. His courage, activity, and zeal was the admiration of myself and all who witnessed it; and when many a veteran looked as if he had just heard his death-warrant, and I felt sick at heart as human blood covered me, spouting from the quivering limbs and mangled bodies around, this youthful tyro, with colour unchanged, and eyes flashing brighter, exposed himself in the most reckless and daring manner to their numerous musketry, and, like the French admiral, escaped unscathed, proving that kind providence frequently shields the brave and destroys the timid.

At this time my friend West fell across my feet with a hideous groan; a large splinter from the mainmast had bared his right thigh bone from the knee-pan to the hip. He lived to reach Palermo, and then sunk under his sufferings. These, with other shocking sights, made me feel sick at heart, and I thought the glorious pomp of war anything but pleasant. I heard the captain exclaim that he was wounded, and in pompous terms desired the quarter-master to bring a chair, which he filled in great state; splinters from the main-mast had struck every person on deck, but fortunately our chief so slightly, that the master afterwards declared that he bound it with a white handkerchief for fear of mistaking the leg.

We were at this time totally unmanageable, and cracking masts and yards in close contact with our foe, who now tried his last effort at boarding. 'Small-arm men and pikemen, forward, to assist boarders!' shouted the chief. 'Request his highness to assemble his troops on the forecastle.' Alas! sorry am I to say, that very few responded to the martial call; and the prince shortly after passed me, covered with the blood of two of our seamen, killed at the cabin guns, his cheeks divested of their roses, and the 'grand desire' filled to satiety.

'Sare,' said his highness, addressing the captain of one of the quarter-deck guns, 'can you tell me where Colonel St. Ange, my aide-de-camp, is gone?'

'I don't know,' said Jack, with great unconcern, replacing an old quid he had just discarded; 'unless you mean the spindle-shanked, hook-nosed fellow I saw with you when the boarders were called for'ard.'

'Ay, ay, he has de Roman nose; where shall I find him?'

'Below,' said Jack.

'Why for he go below?'

'To save his bacon,' quaintly said the sailor; 'heave her breech aft, so – stand clear!' and the gun being fired, rebounded with great velocity.

The dismayed prince, turning to me, asked for an explanation of 'save his bacon.' I with difficulty made him understand that, in the opinion of the captain of the gun, Colonel St. Ange had not consulted his honour in going into a place of safety.

'Have you the place of de safety here?' said the prince.

'What we consider so – where the wounded are dressed,' replied I.

'Sare,' said his highness, raising his hat, 'I will be particularly obligated to you to show me this place of de safety dat you have here.'

'Your highness must excuse my leaving the deck, which I dare not do; but by descending two ladders below this, you will arrive at the cockpit, where I have no doubt you will find Colonel St. Ange.'

It is unnecessary to say that his highness was not visible on deck again during the action, which still raged with unremitting fury. A few thumps increased our distance from each other, and placed us in a raking position for the foe to hammer at.

'It is twenty minutes, sir,' said Mr. Staines, 'since a gun would bear from the lower deck.'

'I am truly sorry to hear it,' said the chief; 'I wish they would all bear.'

'Do order the *Penelope*, sir, to tow us fairly alongside.'

'Here, youngster – the *Penelope's* pendants.'

'We have no means of hoisting them,' said I.

'Don't start difficulties, boy, but hold the tack up on the rail, and I will carry the head up the mizzen-rigging'; and our gallant lieutenant climbed the rigging like a cat.

'Mr. Staines, I command you to come down, and the whole of you off the poop, for the mizzen-mast is falling!' shouted our captain.

There was a rush to obey, and in the struggle I was thrown down with some violence by the long legs of Tom Collins, our tall marine officer. It took me some time to ascertain, first, the safety of my head, and then if I had my proper quantity of limbs left. To my great relief, I found legs, arms, and body untouched, and forthwith proceeded to use them, by scrambling off that slaughter-house of a deck, and out of the way of the falling mizzen-mast, which now came down on the quarter-deck with a horrible crash, breaking through it, and crushing to death the captain of the mizzen-top, a very fine lad, whose father, a quartermaster at the helm, had only a few minutes before been carried down with his right arm shot off. Captain Blackwood had seen our distressed situation under the raking fire of our foe, and his own pendants now approached us.

'I will heave about, and tow you close enough to singe the Frenchman's whiskers.' His foremast, that had been tottering some time, now fell with a thundering noise, and a heartfelt cheer was raised from both ships. Our larboard broadside now bore upon him, and away went his mainmast. 'Work away, my hearts of oak, and his tri-coloured flag will soon be under water,' responded fore and aft; 'though, give the devil his due, he is a good piece of stuff, and merits better than drowning.'

At this time the only sergeant of marines on board (the rest being before Malta), a very gallant man, was borne across the quarter-deck, with his left thigh shot off. The blood played like a fountain, and deluged all within its reach. 'Set me down,' said the wounded man. 'Water, water – oh, give me water!' He drank eagerly, and fell back dead. The body was immediately consigned to the deep; and before I recovered the shock given to my feelings, 'Youngster,' said the captain, 'get me the number of wounded from the surgeon.'

'Ay, ay, sir,' and not particularly sorry for a short respite from such an infernal fire as the *Guillaume Tell* kept on us, both in artillery and small-arms. But when I entered the cockpit, and my optics served me by candlelight from the broad glare of the sun, after stumbling against some of the wounded, I approached the medical tribe, who, with shirt-sleeves tucked up to the shoulders, their hands and arms bathed in human blood, were busily employed in taking the old quarter-master's right arm out of the socket, whose only son, the captain of the mizzen-top, I had just seen crushed to death.

'Is my boy doing well, mister?' addressing me in the low voice of pain.

I felt choking, as I answered, 'I hope he is.'

The old man groaned heavily; he suspected the truth from the tone of my voice.

'Pour a glass of Madeira down his throat – he is sinking fast,' said the surgeon.

The complication of noises in this den of misery – the shrill cry from agonised youth, to the deep and hollow groan of death – the imprecations of some, and the prayers of others – the roaring of guns – and the hopes and fears that pervade the wounded – formed a very shocking scene, and is still deeply impressed on my memory.

'I am too busy to count the wounded,' said the surgeon; 'say the cockpit is full, and some bad cases.'

This I delivered to our chief, seated on his chair in regal dignity, surrounded by young midshipmen, his aides-de-camp.

'I think their fire slackens, Mr. Thompson,' addressing the first lieutenant.

'It evidently does, sir; many of the crew have deserted their guns, and will not relish their admiral's determination to go down with colours flying. He is a brave boy, and fights like an Englishman. The stump of his mainmast is just gone, and nothing can be seen above his bulwarks. Listen to that mutinous cry – the rascals want to strike their colours – the brave admiral is flashing his sabre around it – grape and canister in this gun, and fire on that mutinous gang; for I like discipline, even in an enemy,' said our first lieutenant.

Down came the tri-coloured flag, and 'Cease firing!' resounded along our decks; but one of our lower deck guns gave tongue, and killed their first lieutenant, much praised and lamented by the prisoners, his brother officers. The slaughter on board the *Guillaume Tell* was about four hundred, and in our ship alone eighty, taking in the wounded. Never was any ship better fought, or flag hoisted by a more gallant man than Rear-Admiral Decrés. Our captain received his sword, and took it to the commodore, wearing half a cocked hat, the other half having been carried off by that impudent shot that dyed his cabin with the blood of two seamen, and blanched the bold front of that pretty dandy, the most illustrious the Prince of Palermo.

'Good God! how did you save your head?' said the commodore.

'The hat was not on it,' replied our chief.

Few of the prisoners were removed. The *Penelope* took the prize in two, and one of the sloops ourselves. Completely exhausted both in body and mind, I threw myself down among the wounded, and slept soundly till roused by the cheering of the crew, who had, in the Nelsonian style, been assembled to return thanks to Almighty God, the giver of all victory, and were now applauding their captain's short speech in praise of their conduct, which had not appeared to me extremely commendable; in fact, she was not in a high state of discipline. The men, when threatened with punishment for misconduct, applied to Lady Hamilton, and her kindness of disposition, and Lord Nelson's known aversion to flogging, generally rendered the appeal successful. As an instance of which, one of his bargemen addressed her, in my hearing –

'Please your ladyship's honour, I have got into a bit of a scrawl.'

'What is the nature of it?' said she, with great affability.

'Why, you see, your ladyship's honour, I am reported drunk when on duty yesterday, to the captain, and he will touch me up unless your ladyship's honour interferes. I was not as sober as a judge, because, as why, I was freshish; but I was not drunk.'

'A nice distinction! Let me know what you had drunk.'

'Why, you see, my lady, I was sent ashore after the dinner-grog; and who should I see, on landing, but Tom Mason, from the *Lion*; and Tom says to me, says he, "Jack, let us board this here wine-shop"; so after we had drank a jug, and was making sail for the barge, as steady as an old pump-bolt, in comes Ned, funny Ned – your ladyship's honour recollects Ned, who dances the hornpipe before the king. "My eyes, Jack!" says he; "but we will have another jug, and I'll stand treat," says he; so, you see, wishing to be agreeable like, I takes my share, and the boat waited for me. "You drunken rascal!" says Mr. St. Ives, the middy, to me, "but I'll report you." So I touches my hat, quite genteel like, which shows I was not drunk, and pulls on board without catching crabs; and if your ladyship's honour will tell the admiral that I pulled on board without catching crabs, he will see with half an eye that I only shook a cloth in the wind.'

'Your name,' said 'Fair Emma,' taking out her tablets.

'Jack Jones; and God bless that handsome face, for it is the sailor's friend.'

And Jack, hitching up his trousers, gave a scrape with his foot, and bounded off with a light heart, well knowing the powerful influence he had moved in his favour would save his back from severe flagellation. She was much liked by everyone in the fleet, except Captain Nesbit, Lady Nelson's son; and her recommendation was the sure road to promotion. The fascination of her elegant manners was irresistible, and her voice most melodious. Bending her graceful form over her superb harp, on the *Foudroyant's* quarter-deck each day after dinner, in Naples' Bay, she sang the praises of Nelson, at which the hero blushed like a fair maiden listening to the first compliment paid to her beauty.

THE ROYAL VISIT

The *Foudroyant*, with her prize, was towed into Syracuse harbour. Arrived at Palermo, and Lord Nelson's flag again decorating our mizzen-top-gallant mast, all Sicily flocked on board to compliment the gallant men who had brought in a foe so dreaded. The royal standard, seen in the admiral's barge, and the long measured stroke of the rowers, with the respectful standing position of the lieutenant at the helm, denote that the very highest in the realm are on board. The boatswain's shrill pipe called attention; and the words, 'All hands man ship, ahoy!' re-echoed by his mates through the different decks, instantly placed seven hundred men in our rigging, the light top-men, that were to ascend the dizzy height of the royal yards in advance. 'Away, aloft!' and like a flash of lightning, they ascend to their respective posts; the graceful toss of the bowman's oar, and the tune from the boatswain's call, gave the signal to 'lay out,' and our well-squared yards were covered by sailors in their long-quartered shoes, check shirt, blue jacket, and trousers white as driven snow, with queues hanging down their backs, for cropping was not then in fashion, while three bold and active boys climbed the royal masts, and sat on the trucks apparently much at ease.

'Turn out a captain's guard, summon all the officers, and six of the best-dressed midshipmen attend the side ropes, and plant the silk standard in the ladies' chair,' into which the hero of England and the pride of the navy awkwardly (from the want of an arm) assisted the Queen of Sicily and her three daughters. 'Whip handsomely, and bear her off, young gentlemen;' and the daughter of Maria Theresa, with animated eyes and a quick step, advanced to the captain, who gallantly kissed her fair hand, while she, with great volubility, complimented and thanked him over and over again; and turning to the officers with inimitable grace, she and her daughters presented hands to be kissed by each and all of us. For my part, I was so enraptured by the striking beauty of one of the princesses, that my salute was ardent, and the pressure accorded with my feeling – for I was completely in the seventh heaven – and long did that soft pressure and kiss dwell on my fancy, and haunt my slumbers. The band played a march, the guard presented arms, and the officers uncovered, as the descendant of Maria Theresa placed her foot on the deck of the conqueror's ship, the Sicilian royal standard displayed at the main, the unfolding of whose banners roused the sleeping thunder of the squadron. A royal salute welcomed this energetic woman, whose slender and perfect form seemed to tread on air, while the tender animation of her sparkling eyes expressed a warmth of heart that prompted her (at least in my imagination) to embrace all around her. Very little time did she devote to the splendid collation prepared for her; but with her amiable daughters, sought to soothe the anguish of pain, and alleviate the sufferings of the wounded. The drums beat to arms, and the court inspected the quarters on their way to the different hospitals established in the ship; with every wounded man and boy they shook hands, saying something kind and consoling, while their gifts were munificent. The princesses shed tears over the sufferings they beheld, and enclosed their delicate hands in the iron grasp of Jack, as he lay restless on his couch of pain; but still he was an object of envy to me, as the beauteous Marie Antoinette bent over him with looks of pity that an angel might have envied, while her coral lips gave utterance to the most melodious sounds that ever extracted the sting from the anguish of the suffering, either in mind or body. The last object of attention to the royal party was my excellent friend and brother signal-midshipman, Mr. West, the chaplain making way for us. Here was a change, shocking to behold; the fine apple-cheeked, bold boy had shrunk into a withered, and apparently old man, by his sufferings; fevered, emaciated, and wan, he lay a ghastly spectacle. Lord Nelson, with great feeling, took him by the hand, praised his courage, told him he was promoted by him, and hailed him as Lieutenant West. No emotion was shown by the heroic boy, no other word was uttered by him than 'drink'; the young princess, with great promptitude, divided an orange, and squeezed the juice on his parched lips. Lord Nelson introduced the Queen of Naples and her fair daughters as mourning his misfortunes, in which in truth they took a deep interest as they stood by his cot in tears; he exhorted him to look forward to long life and high rank in his profession; the surgeon shook his head and whispered, an hour was the utmost tenure he held of this world, as the wound had gangrened. The good-natured hero seemed much shocked, and showed great emotion. The boy, finding relief and gratification from the kind exertions of the princess, opened his eyes with a death-like stare as she bent over him; at once he seemed to comprehend his situation; the blood again rallied to the heart; the pulse that had nearly ceased again resumed its beat; animation lighted up his eyes. As he surveyed the beautiful vision he no doubt thought of his far distant home and its affectionate inmates. I heard him audibly sigh, and saw him make a feeble attempt to kiss the fair hand that had so kindly administered to his wants. It was the last effort of expiring nature; the gallant boy dropped on his pillow – his fine eyes assumed the glazed hue of death – the rattles in the throat gave notice of the difficulty of respiration, and the surgeon announced him to be in his last agonies. Here was a lesson of mortality to a frivolous and dissolute court! The maids of honour, and the officers of the household, walked off without waiting for orders, first attempting in vain to move the queen and princesses, who evinced deep feeling, and the sobs of the lovely young princess were quite hysterical. Lord Nelson in silent grief motioned Lady Hamilton to remove the queen, and with the Princess Royal on his only arm, led the way on deck. Our gallant captain gave an arm to each of the younger princesses, and the royal procession embarked in his barge in solemn silence, so different from the animation and pleasure that had lighted up their expressive features on their arrival. The guard had been dismissed, the band ceased to play, and silence was ordered fore and aft on the knowledge of my friend's fate. The gallant boy was interred with military honours in the ground of the Protestant chapel of the ambassador. He died the death of a hero, and sincerely mourned by his brother officers, and was long remembered for his good qualities by those who had the pleasure of knowing him. Peace to his *manes*!

THE NELSONIAN BALL

The wounded and sick were landed with the utmost tenderness, and well looked after on shore. The gallant ship purified, the flags floated gaily from their usual stations, and all appearance of sorrow was dismissed. Now were notes of great preparation for a splendid dinner and ball, to be given by Lord Nelson, to commemorate two great events – the capture of *La Guillaume Tell* (the only ship that escaped from the battle of the Nile that was not one of our own), and the marriage of the Prime Minister of Naples, 'Sir John Acton,' a tall, spare Scotchman, bent by age, being on the wrong side of seventy, to a beautiful girl (his niece) on the right side of twelve, though her appearance was not so juvenile as her years: this abominable sacrifice of youth, innocence, and beauty was made at the altar of Mammon. By raising the awnings twenty feet, removing the guns, and robing the masts in silk, two spacious rooms were given, and these were most splendidly decorated; and when lighted up in the evening, really presented a very fairylike appearance, while the music that floated over the calm waters of this beautiful bay was softened. All the nobles of the court, with the exception of the king and queen, were there; the Marquis de Neeza, admiral of the Portuguese squadron, accompanied by his officers, gave a light-some appearance, and took from the sombre hue thrown by Mustapha Bey and the Turkish grandees. The captive French admiral[2] also excited great and deserved attention, and on his health being given by his conqueror, made a concise speech, in which he highly complimented Captain Blackwood, and told Lord Nelson that to that brave man alone he was indebted to the capture of *La Guillaume Tell*; and, to impress us with the idea of his estima-tion of him, embraced him French fashion, by kissing each of his cheeks. We all perceived, by the heightened colour, that the gallant Blackwood would willingly have dispensed with the fraternal hug – especially when complimented by his youthful brother officers on this undesired instance of the Frenchman's admiration. The youth-ful part of the select guests arrived in groups alongside the flagship, whose brilliant illumination lighted the whole bay. When two young scions of a princely house arrived in their well-appointed barge, one of our lieutenants, who had sacrificed freely to the jolly god, excited by wine and beauty – for one of the princesses was really handsome – rushed to offer his services as became a gallant knight; but I am glad to say, was anticipated with the beauty by a brother officer, who had not drunk all the given toasts in bumpers. Rather heated, he incautiously assisted the sister, whose temper, like her person, was capable of improvement, and, in his drunken efforts, plunged both into the water. The musical screams of numerous lovely throats were heard in various intonations. The well-washed princess, in her drenched feathers and finery, was brought on deck, and appeared a sea-nymph of the fury kind. She demanded that the unfortunate hero, who was making drunken apologies, should be immediately hanged at the foreyard arm. To this our hero, with his usual aversion to punishment, demurred; asserting that English law, both civil and military, did not allow of such summary justice; but he pacified the enraged fair one by plac-ing the offending officer under an arrest; and Lady Hamilton, in a

2 Admiral Decrés, who eventually became Minister of the French Marine, was murdered by his own servant in Paris, a few years afterwards.

short time, produced the fury, dressed, but with more taste, under her kind inspection. Now commenced the graceful and animated dance of the Saltarella, far different from our sleepy way of walking, like mutes at a funeral, through the quadrilles, where each is determined to act the statue – the elastic spring of the deck being the greater from the supporting stanchions being withdrawn. The animation and vivid feelings of the beaux – the voluptuous and graceful forms of the senoras – the glances of their expressive black eyes, and their raven tresses, were very striking; but all this, beautiful as it really was, did not (in my opinion) outvie the modest lily of England, in the youthful Baroness of Acton. I have heard she is still a very fine woman. Her husband was a good-natured man, with whom I have often conversed, particularly on one occasion that now occurs to my memory. Two very fine calves had been presented to his Majesty, in Naples Bay, dressed as female fashionables of the highest grade – viz., in satin, with ostrich feathers on their heads, which they tossed about as if proud of all the finery they were loaded with. This unusual mode of clothing calves pleased the king, and threw us into uncontrollable laughter. Sir John told us, in a kind way, to look at the motive, which was loyalty to a beneficent sovereign, and not to attach so much ridicule to the act. Some strange circumstances attended the funeral of this respected old gentleman; but as I was not an eye-witness, I forbear to detail newspaper reports that might wound the feelings of his beautiful and amiable widow.

Some few of the dancers had ventured to brave the beams of the rising sun, while the judicious, fully aware that rouged cheeks and uncurled tresses do not make the impressions that all female hearts desire to make, had retired some hours before, accompanying the admiral and ambassadors.

The following day we were ordered to prepare to receive her Majesty the Queen of Naples, and her three daughters, to convey them to Leghorn, on their passage to the Court of Vienna; a seventy-four and a frigate were also ordered to receive their suites and baggage.

THE ROYAL PARTY

My Lord Nelson in person took command of the squadron, and the king escorted his energetic partner and daughters on board, and was received with the greatest honours paid to crowned heads. Shortly after he reached our quarter-deck, Lord Nelson's favourite servant, the well-known Tom Allen, formerly a waister in the *Agamemnon*, in a broad Norfolk dialect, asked his Majesty of the Two Sicilies how he did. The king, fully aware of the liberty this spoilt domestic took, very graciously presented his hand to be kissed, which the other shook heartily, saying, 'How do you do, Mr. King?' to the amusement of all the spectators, save his lordship, who ineffectually attempted to polish his rough Norfolk caste. This man, who had a feeling heart under a very rough exterior, was ordered by Lord Nelson, on the 14th of February, to ask every officer that had been in the gallant action off St. Vincent, to dinner. I was honoured by Tom with the usual invite. 'You must dine with his lordship to-day.'

'Very sorry I cannot, Tom.'

'You must.'

'I have no clean shirt, and my messmates are in the same plight.'

Away Tom bustled up to the admiral, who good-naturedly said I might dine in any shirt, but must celebrate the anniversary of that glorious and unprecedented victory at his table at three o'clock that day. This was the first time I dined with the heroic Nelson, whose manners to his inferiors were most conciliatory and kind, his smile inimitable, and when he asked me to take wine from his own bottle, the produce of the grape grown in his dukedom of Bronté, I thought he looked very handsome, though at times his face was melancholy, betraying a mind ill at ease. Five glasses of wine were all the admiral could bear, and Tom Allen led him away, reminding him of his sufferings on the following day from the least excess. The passage of the royal party to Leghorn was effected in turbulent weather; the two eldest of the princesses gave way to the debility caused by sea-sickness, while the lovely sister, with all the energy of the queen-mother, combated the effects of this nauseous disorder. Her hearty laugh at the efforts she ineffectually made through the speaking trumpet to converse with the ladies of the court as the squadron crowded under our stern, still dwells in my memory; for there is an inexpressible delight in the ringing laugh of childhood, when the whole heart seems filled with joy. The queen and her family shed pearly tears, as the crew cheered them on their leaving, and the thunder of the Tuscany cannon announced that the royal family of Naples had landed in the grand duke's territories. The *Foudroyant* and the squadron made sail for Malta, that still continued in siege and starvation. Lady Hamilton either felt, or affected to feel, extremely grieved at parting with the queen and family; and to cheer her profound sorrow, Miss Knight[3] composed the following song on the trophies hung in Lord Nelson's cabin –

'Come, cheer up, fair Emma, forget all thy grief,
Your shipmates are brave, and a hero's their chief;
Look around on these trophies, the pride of the main,
They were snatch'd by their valour from Gallia and Spain.
    Hearts of oak are our ships, hearts of oak are our men,
        We always are ready,
        Steady, boys, steady,
    To fight and to conquer again and again!
'These arms the *San Josef* once claim'd as her own,
Till Nelson and Britons their pride had o'erthrown;
That plume, too, evinces that still they excel –
'Twas torn from the cap of the famed *Guillaume Tell.*
    Hearts of oak, etc.

'Behold yonder trophy, 'tis sacred to fame,
From Nile's olden wave it was saved from the flame –
That flame which destroy'd all the glory of France,
When Providence conquer'd the friends of blind chance.
    Hearts of oak, etc.

'Then cheer up, fair Emma, remember thou'rt free,
And ploughing Britannia's old empire, the sea;
How many in Albion each sorrow would check,
Could they kiss but one plank of this conquering deck!
    Hearts of oak are our ships, hearts of oak are our men,
        We always are ready,
        Steady, boys, steady,
    To fight and to conquer again and again!'

[3] Daughter of Admiral Sir Joseph Knight. She accompanied Lord Nelson and Sir W. and Lady Hamilton to England in 1800. She afterwards was sub-governess to H.R.H. the Princess Charlotte. She was the authoress of several works, and died in 1839.

THE CRUISE

Lady Hamilton's grief produced its concomitant effects upon her frame, for the mind and body are too closely allied not to sympathise with each other. She was pronounced ill by Esculapius, and perfect silence prevailed. Stillness was observed in all parts of this Noah's ark, save and except the infernal regions, where the jolly reefers held their carouse, and played all manner of boyish pranks with impunity. I can truly aver that there is more happiness to be found in these dip-lighted abodes than in the splendid cabin or wardroom. Divested of all responsibility, the midshipman enjoys the present day without a thought of the morrow. Our black servant (a prince by his own account), acting in the capacity of steward, cook, and butler, was brought up before a self-constituted court, and charged with stealing from divers midshipmen (his then masters) their pots of pomatum. This loss was the more serious, as a cauliflower head was in those days the distinguishing mark of loyalty. The case was proved to an amazing extent, as not a particle of that indispensable was left in the mess, and the purser's dips suffered as substitutes accordingly. 'Colonel Crib' (a nick-name given to the worthy president, from being strongly marked with that foe to beauty the smallpox) called on the black prince for his defence, which is rather ingenious – 'that massa had the whole of his pomatum back in the different made dishes that massa buckra praised so highly.' This excited both nausea and anger in his judges, who reflected with dismay on their delight in the savoury dishes his highness had so concocted. Punishment followed closely on the sentence, which was fifty strokes with the sheath of a sword on the shin bones, the most susceptible place about a black, which the prince endured with the stoicism of a martyr.

But having digressed into the boyish pranks of a cockpit, I must return to a more serious subject (at least, in Lord Nelson's opinion), the illness of Lady Hamilton, who was very feverish; and to give her rest, the *Foudroyant* was run off before the wind, with her yards braced by, for the whole night, which had the desired effect; for to his great joy – and, indeed, it gave pleasure to all on board – she was pronounced convalescent. I have said but very little of the husband of this extraordinary woman; but as he lived with her on board, I must now introduce him. He was a spare, gentlemanly old man, kind to every person and much beloved. Of the goodness of his disposition I experienced a rare and striking instance. One noon, enticed by the savoury smell of the viands that his highness was bearing to our table, I followed them down, fully aware that the last comer was not the best served. Just as I, with great haste, had scalded my mouth with a piece of plum-pudding – for, observe, gentle reader, the plums are barely within hail of each other – the quarter-deck messenger announced that Sir Edward was on deck, and wanted the signal-midshipman. Ye gods! how I scampered up the ladder, and by the greatest ill-luck encountered Sir William Hamilton[4] tottering down with all the caution of age. The concussion was dreadful, and I stood bewildered and aghast! I had overthrown the representative of majesty, and seriously hurt his back against the steps of the companion ladder. Hanging and all sorts of punishment flitted across my imagination. Before I could apologise or recover myself, the old man rose from the recumbent position I had so unceremoniously placed him in, and with a voice of kindness, patted me on the head, with a request that I would keep a better look-out afore when called upon for similar haste. I did not find my commander so placable as the ambassador, for he not only sent me to the masthead, but ordered that I should keep watch and watch there for a week. Lady Hamilton, with her usual kindness, got the latter part of the sentence remitted.

During the passage, we encountered a thunderstorm, and the electric fluid struck away our foretopmast, killing one man and wounding fourteen. The *Principo Real*, a Portuguese ship of the line, lost her mainmast that night from the same cause, with several men killed. Having shifted the topmast, we arrived off Lavalette, that impregnable capital of Malta, and anchored close within the mouth of the harbour to prevent any supplies being thrown in. Famine prevailed in the town to such an extent, that the only thing found in *La Guillaume Tell* was the leg of a mule, hung for safety and his especial use over the admiral's stern-galley. The expectation of an early surrender, formed upon this known state of destitution, I imagined influenced Lord Nelson, the ambassador, and his lady

[4] Sir W. Hamilton was the son of Lord Archibald Hamilton, and grandson of William, third Duke of Hamilton. He was born in 1730, was English Ambassador at Naples from 1764 to 1800, married his second wife, Emma Lyon, in 1791, and died 1803.

(she being the only female knight of Malta in the world, the honour having been conferred on her by the Russian Emperor Paul) to hope that they might be present at the surrender. But we were all disappointed, for a young officer, a relation of his lordship, having the watch the first night of our arrival, very quietly composed himself to sleep, with an injunction to the mate to rouse him if necessary. A breeze unexpectedly came in from the sea, and the ship dragged her anchor. Davis, the mate, kicked his feet with information of this event; but the luff (according to a phrase used in those days) was as easy as 'Jack Easy.'

'Dragging her anchor, is she, Davis? Oh, then, give her cable.'

'She has brought up, Mr. ***,' reported the mate.

'I thought she would,' said the sleeper.

'But I have a notion within gunshot of the fort,' said the mate.

'Well,' replied the careless luff, disencumbering himself from his cloak, 'I must report this.' And giving a loud yawn, he awoke Sir Edward.

'Very well, Mr. ***, we will shift our berth at daylight.'

'Ay, ay, sir,' said our careless friend, and then resumed his nap.

Hunger, I suppose, kept the Frenchman waking, and at peep of day he made us a target for all his sea batteries to practise on. 'All hands up' – 'Anchor ahoy!' resounded fore and aft, and we hove short to the music of the shot, some of them going far over us.

Lord Nelson was in a towering passion, and Lady Hamilton's refusal to quit the quarter-deck did not tend to tranquilise him. When short a-peak, the breeze failed, leaving only its disagreeable concomitant – a swell.

'Hoist out the launch, and carry out your stream anchor, Sir Ed'ard.'

'Very well, my lord.'

'And, youngster,' said his lordship, 'take the cutter on board the *Success*, and bring Captain Peard to me.'

Just at this moment a shot from Long Tom of Malta, now to be seen in St. James's Park, struck the unfortunate fore-topmast, inflicting a deadly wound. His lordship then insisted upon Lady Hamilton's retiring, who did not evince the same partiality for the place of 'de safety' as our illustrious friend the Prince of Palermo, and leaving them in high altercation, I proceeded to his Majesty's frigate *Success*.

Captain Peard, who had anticipated such a summons, came into the boat, in full uniform, as is usual, when waiting on the commander-in-chief. The captain of Long Tom of Malta, spying the gold-laced hat and epaulets, sent a shot a long way outside of us. Again he treated us with one that splashed equal to a moderate shower; the third struck within us, and bounded over in most musical style, and it passed near enough to our heads to cause a disagreeable sensation. The coxswain was particularly alive to the emotion, and fell over Captain Peard and myself in the stern sheets, carrying me, who made little opposition, under him. 'Where are you wounded, my man?' said the captain, in a voice of kindness. But when he found that the nerves alone suffered, in a harsh tone he ordered the coxswain into his box, and sat unmoved. He was, in truth, an honour to the navy, and merited a better fate.

After sustaining a severe fire, we warped out of gunshot, and again had to replace the fore-topmast. And Lady Hamilton, finding that the French governor would not surrender until he had made a meal of his shoes, influenced Lord Nelson to turn her head for Palermo, a much more agreeable place, and where the balls were not all of iron. On our passage we fell in with the *Queen Charlotte* bearing a vice-admiral's flag, and found it to be Lord Keith come to supersede our hero. This caused many long faces on our quarter-deck, and even Lord Nelson's countenance wore an expression of vexation as he arrayed himself in his paraphernalia of stars and diamonds to wait on his senior officer. The conference was short. The successor to the ambassador, Sir Arthur Paget, was likewise on board, and our head was turned towards Leghorn, where we landed the hero of the Nile and the explorer of Vesuvius, with Lady Hamilton. We shortly after received the flag of Lord Keith, owing to the unfortunate destruction of the *Queen Charlotte* by fire, a few hours after she had quitted the Leghorn roads, which the following letters will explain:–

Leaves from Memory's Log

THE BURNING SHIP

'My dear friend, – Ere now you have heard of the lamentable catastrophe of the old *Charlotte*, and the miraculous preservation of your friend. I will, as far as I can collect my ideas, give you a faint description of the horrid scene that keeps my brain in a whirl of agitation, and will ever remain while memory holds her seat. With many of the officers I was on shore at Leghorn, intending to accompany a large party to the opera, when a rumour reached me that the ship was ordered to sea, under Captain Todd. Upon this I walked to the admiral's palazzio, and received notice to join instantly, as she was then unmooring. With a few, hastily collected, we repaired on board, leaving many young midshipmen, that had strayed away, God knows where, ashore, found the ship a stay peak, and heard the "Pipe all hands – make sail, ahoy – let fall – sheet home and hoist away," and our beautifully cut canvas stretched upon our square yards, decorated our taper masts, with the celerity of a well-organised ship, thick and dry for weighing. "Brace the yards for casting to starboard," said Captain Todd; "and heave and a-weigh." The drums and fifes struck up "Coil away the hawser," and the measured tramp of the men gave life and jollity to the scene, and was an excellent accompaniment to the heart-inspiring tune. "She is a-weigh, sir," said the officer of the forecastle to the first lieutenant, as the noble ship fell gracefully off to starboard, who, returning the salute, reported the same to the captain; and he, pacing the deck, looked a noble sea officer of large proportions. And now, to reflect that that godlike form is reduced to ashes, the muscles that gave herculean strength to the goodly fabric shrivelled to nothing by intense heat, the very bones calcined, and the whole shapeless mass of ashes buried in the ocean's depth – but I am anticipating. At four that morning, having kept the middle watch, I left the goodly ship under her courses and top-gallant sails "ploughing the waters like a thing of life," a breeze having just sprung up, as she had been becalmed most of the night. The lighthouse was full in view and not far distant. At six I was awoke from a deep sleep by the firing of guns that, from their contiguity, shook my cot. Alarmed at such an unusual circumstance, and with the hurried feet of men running to and fro, I made to the wardroom door, upon opening which, a dense volume of thick black smoke drove me back, half-suffocated and bewildered. I ran to the weather-quarter gallery; and there, O God! what a sight burst on my view! The flames that rose from the quarter-deck, and gave it the appearance of the crater of a volcano, had just reached the mainsail; their glare was reflected strongly on the agitated faces of hundreds of men assembled on the forecastle. "There is Dundas," said Lieutenant Erskine to me, for he had joined me in his shirt, in the quarter-gallery; "there is Dundas, on the forecastle, endeavouring to let go the anchors; I will join him or perish."

"'Better join the launch," said I, which, full of men, was making her best efforts, with only one oar, to increase her distance from the burning ship. Amidst the roar of artillery and the cries of despair, I heard the manly tones of Captain Todd's voice over my head; what he said I could not make out; but poor Erskine, who was immoderately fat for a lieutenant, made his ascent to the quarter-deck bulwarks, along which he was climbing. The ship lurched to leeward, the bulwarks gave way with a horrid crash, and disclosed what might have passed for the mouth of hell, into which my poor friend was hurried in an instant. I heard his agonised cry, as the flame, like the tongue of a serpent, lapped him in its folds; I saw his last despairing glance thrown upon me, and the bright glow of the furnace threw a more lurid glare as it enveloped him. O God! it was a sickening sight! The sea was covered with struggling sailors; the few boats that ventured near, under a heavy fire which the guns, that were all shotted, sent forth, were full to sinking. Some of our young midshipmen were in these boats, and forced the cowardly Italians into the fire at the point of their dirks. Both anchors were now cut away, and the noble ship swung head to the wind in consequence. I found my post much incommoded by the smoke and flames that were now blown aft, and with the short ejaculation used by the publican and sinner, which came from my heart, I plunged into the water, and struck out for the launch.

"'There is no room, and we cannot take you in," said many voices from the boat. "Keep off, on your peril!" said a discordant

one, as I grasped the gunnel of the well-filled boat, and a heavy
blow broke two of the fingers of my right hand, and made me
relinquish my hold. I then swam alongside the boat, and entreated
them to save me. Though a few, with the generous quality that
characterises British seamen, would have risked the safety of the
boat in my favour, still the majority were against me; and the
ruffian who had disabled my hand sat watching me, ready to repeat
the blow. To depict my feelings in this tremendous scene! – they
can be imagined, but not described. Under the stern of the burning
ship, that was discharging her hundred and thirty guns, were seen
hundreds of men, swimming and floating on spars; in the distance,
vessels afraid of venturing near the shot and expected explosion of
the magazines; here and there a few Italian boats, with a young
midshipman, at the point of his dirk, urging them to save the
drowning; one or two from English merchantmen, regardless of all
danger, loading with the swimmers, and dashing into the mouth of
danger to receive those who, unable to swim, had hung on the blazing ship to the last. The flames now shot high above the masthead,
and reminded me of an eruption I had once viewed of Etna. It was
very terrible, joined to the cries of the young, the groans of the
wounded, and the shouts and yelling of the burning. Finding
myself much exhausted, I struck out for a man I saw on a grating.
"Hallo, shipmate!" said he, "keep clear, for it is too small for both of
us; boat ahoy!" hailing one of the English ones; "boat ahoy! if you
have room for a spare hand, pick up this poor devil; as for me, I am
doing well, and shall make the Isle of Gorgona in three hours."
Upon which, he spread his neckerchief with his teeth and hands as
a sail, and squatted on the grating apparently at his ease.

'As I was giving up hope, which in general is slow to desert me,
the boat, which the captain of the after-guard of the starboard
watch – for it was the veteran John Nailor that had pointed me out
for succour – hauled me in just in time to prevent me from sinking,
for I had struggled with many a drowning wretch, who clutched
me, as men in that state will, and in consequence I had imbibed a
quantity of water. I was roused from my torpid state by the blowing
up of the after magazine, which detached the whole of her stern-
frame from the body of the now splendid luminary, that gave an
idea of a world in conflagration. She now majestically raised her
bows high in air, with her tapering, lofty masts, and submerged her

stern, going down gracefully in the "deep, deep sea." Every cry was hushed, and people held their breath, as this beautiful fabric of human creation buried itself in the waves, and created an immense commotion in the agitated waters. A tremendous concussion followed, and "Stand clear!" was shouted from the overloaded boats, as the mainmast descended from the immense height to which it was blown by the grand magazine exploding under water; had it taken place above, nothing could have survived the concussion. Down it came, with a horrible crash, tearing all before it, and put an end to the miseries of a hundred half-drowned wretches.'

My dear friend – You will see by the above that I am partially recovering from the extreme depression caused by the horrid calamity detailed in my last. That dreadful scene of conflagration is ever before my eyes, and my nervous system (if sailors are allowed to have nerves) will take some time to recover the shock. I still see the falling of our poor friend Lieutenant Erskine into the blazing furnace, reflecting a strong light on his agitated countenance, as he turned it full upon me, filled with indescribable horror – the piercing and agonised shriek, to which I involuntarily responded, is for ever ringing in my ears – the darting of the forked flames, from yard to yard and mast to mast, till they soared above the clouds and illuminated the most minute object, making all as distinct as the meridian sun – the numberless sinking and struggling sailors – their despairing imprecations when beaten off from the already overloaded boats. One of them, I am told, in a violent paroxysm of madness, before he jumped overboard, deliberately broke the thigh bones of a boy, and threw him into the boiling waters. You will recollect our old messmate, young Smithers, the doctor's son; nearly exhausted, he caught at, and grasped an oar, pulled by a person we both knew without much esteeming. This person, I am informed, cruelly shook him off to certain destruction, and flew to save a much greater man, whom he had seen lower himself from the bowsprit. He was successful, and I have no doubt promotion will be his reward. The last sight of poor Captain Todd was on the poop. He then, half-clad, had pistols in his hands, preventing the quarter cutters from being lowered, and endeavouring to drive the men, intent on escape, to their duty. Poor gentleman! he was a gallant and good man, and fell a victim to the all-devouring flames.

'The cause of this calamity is, I believe, truly stated – that the ship being ordered so suddenly to sea obliged them to press the hay intended for the cabin and wardroom stock, all night. When daylight broke, our old shipmate Robinson, called by us, as you will recollect, Bonaparte, from his dashing appearance, and wearing his cocked hat fore and aft, like a midshipman with money in both pockets, being mate of the morning watch, commenced washing the main deck. Having swabbed the larboard side, he directed the loose hay to be moved over from the starboard, in order that it might go through the same process. In the hurry of moving, it was crowded on the match-tub, in which was the lighted match, placed under the sentinel's charge at the admiral's cabin door (every night one being so placed), without observing the match. It soon burnt into a blaze, and the quarter-deck was in flames before any check could be given. This confined the captain and wardroom officers abaft, and the only one on the forecastle was the Hon. L. Dundas, lately one of the Lords Commissioners of the Admiralty, who let go the anchors, and kept the fire from spreading forward by the ship's swinging head to wind; therefore most of the men saved were on the forecastle. Had it been an English port, as we were not far from it, many more would have escaped with life. But the Italians were afraid of the shot that were dropping in all directions, as the ship swung, and looked on prudence as the better part of valour. They had likewise a well-founded horror of our magazines, that could not be flooded, and which blew the lower masts high into the air, occasioning great destruction to the half-drowned and struggling swimmers. I am told that, as Lord Keith, after sending out every-thing from the mole that was fit for sea, stood on the outer battery, and through his glass saw the destruction of his noble ship, the finest in the British navy, the burning of his gallant captain, Lieutenant Bainbridge, and other officers, with hundreds of his men, his feelings quite unmanned him; and the big tears which coursed each other down his aged cheeks, with his convulsive sobs, attested the acuteness of his sufferings. He is a kind and amiable man, and has lost about six thousand pounds in plate and stock. But you will have an opportunity of judging for yourself, as the *Foudroyant* is intended to take his flag; when, my dear friend, we shall have opportunity for many a long yarn on this melancholy subject, which is always uppermost in my thoughts. Would to God

I could forget the heart-breaking sights I was then a spectator of! they haunt me even in sleep.[1] Yours, ever truly,   ******.'

THE GALE

In the latter end of the month of January, 1801, the day dawned with every indication of bad weather – the mass of dense and heavy clouds, piled upon each other, occupied all space to the south-west – the sun in his course looked with a fiery aspect – and the sea-fowl, with the wonderful instinct that puzzles the wise, from their fore-knowledge of the storm, came screaming in upon the land; the wind blew fiercely, and in fearful gusts – the labouring clouds seemed preparing to discharge their overloaded breasts, and distant thunder rolled along the horizon; the masses of clouds, as they sailed along the ocean, nearly shut out the light of day, and rose at opposite extremities into huge mountains of vapour. They were illuminated by fitful flashes of lightning, and looked like giant batteries erected in the heavens. As they moved onwards from the south-west, they shot down vivid streams, which, at times, pierced the waters like quivering blades of fire; again the electric fluid took an horizontal direction through the skies, and its dazzling streak fluttered like a radiant streamer, until it lost itself among the clouds. Comparative darkness came on with a suddenness that I never before had observed, and the gusts of wind were terrific. During this elemental war, the British fleet under Vice-Admiral Lord Keith, and the army under Sir Ralph Abercrombie, closely crammed in men-of-war (*armes en flûte*), and transports to the number of two hundred sail, were carrying a heavy press of canvas to claw off a lee-shore. That shore was Caramania, in Asia Minor, a most mountainous, well-wooded, black-looking coast. We were in search of Marmorice harbour, the appointed rendezvous of the Egyptian expedition; and the Asiatic pilots, frightened at the dangerous position of the fleet in this tremendous weather, lost the little knowledge they had formerly possessed of this unfrequented and frowning coast, whose mountains towered high above the clouds, and on which no vestige of human life could be seen. Every glass, in the clearance between the squalls, was eagerly turned upon the precipitous shore, upon which the heavy waves beat with most

[1] This appalling catastrophe happened 17th March 1800, about three or four leagues from Leghorn. Only 156 men were saved out of a crew of about 830.

horrific grandeur. It was self-evident to the meanest capacity, that unless the harbour could be entered before night, the transports filled with British warriors would be wrecked on the lee-shore, with no chance of assistance. The men-of-war, by dint of carrying sail, might claw off; but the great majority of this fine army would, in a few hours, become food for the monsters of the deep, or the ferocious and ravenous tenants of the vast forests, that seemed interminable to our straining sight. As each withdrew his glass, with a disappointed look, the longitude of their countenances increased, and the round-faced, laughing midshipman lost his disposition for fun and frolic, and all at once became a reflecting, sedate personage.

The admiral, on whom all the responsibility rested, endeavoured to assume the calmness of tone and manner that the honesty of his open nature would not brook; his agitiation was visible in the contortions of his venerable countenance, and the sudden starts of his nervous system. 'Fire a gun, and hoist a signal of attention to the fleet,' said his lordship.

'They have all answered, my lord,' said the officer of the signal department.

'Now, Mr. Staines, be particular; ask if anyone is qualified to lead into Marmorice.'

As the negative flag flew at the masthead of the men-of-war, every countenance proportionally fell. At length, with heartfelt joy, I proclaimed that one of our sloops had hoisted her affirmative.

'Who is she, youngster? Boy, do not keep me in suspense.'

'The *Petrel*, my lord.'

I saw an ejaculation of thankfulness rise warm from the heart to the lips of Lord Keith, as he piously raised his eyes and pressed his hand on his heart. 'Signal for the fleet to bear up, make more sail, and follow the *Petrel*,' said Lord Keith. '*Captain Inglis may be depended on.*' And we shook out a reef, and set the main-top-gallant sail, which soon closed our leader in the *Petrel*. As we approached this mountainous and novel land, the idea (and it was an astounding one) seemed to dwell on and occupy the most unreflecting mind, that should Captain Inglis be wrong, every ship, with twenty-five thousand men, would be the sacrifice of such error. Lord Keith ordered the signal of attention with the *Petrel's* pendants. 'Captain Inglis, your responsibility is awful,' said the telegraph. 'Are you perfectly certain of the entrance of Marmorice?'

'Perfectly sure,' said the answer; 'and right ahead.'

'Signal officers on the foreyard, with their glasses,' said the admiral; and slinging our telescopes, we ascended. Indeed it was time; for now the roar of the waves, as they broke on the coast, throwing their spray on high, conveyed a dismal idea of our impending fate.

'A narrow entrance ahead!' called the signal-lieutenant Staines.

'Do the midshipmen make out the same?'

'We all of us discern it, my lord,' shouted the whole at the very extent of our voices.

'God be praised for this great mercy!' ejaculated his lordship, uncovering and bowing his head with great devotion; and I do aver and believe that the grateful sentiment pervaded every heart in the *Foudroyant*.

The entrance of Marmorice now became distinctly visible to all on deck, from the contrast of the deep, still water to the creamy froth on the shore; and the signal for the convoy to crowd all sail for the port in view, and the men-of-war to haul their wind, until the merchantmen had entered the channel, was flying at the *Foudroyant's* masthead, as she shot into the gut of Marmorice. The tremendous mountains overshadowed us, and seemed inclined, from their great height, to come thundering down upon us like the destructive avalanches in the mountains of Switzerland. We now entered the spacious and splendid harbour, circular in its form, and more than twenty miles in circumference. It created great astonishment from its vast magnitude, seeming capable of containing all the ships in the world, with its mountainous shore and immense forests. In so small a nook as to be nearly invisible, stands on a rock a fort, and a few wretched houses, surrounded by a high wall, I conjecture for the purpose of keeping out the wild beasts, which seemed here lords of the ascendant. This fortification displayed the Crescent, and was saluted with eleven guns, as we took up anchorage, closely followed by our numerous fleet. Scarcely had we moored, when the heavy masses of clouds that had rested on and capped the high land, now opened upon us in earnest, and the forked lightnings darted among the fleet with fatal effect. The gale increased to a perfect hurricane, and blew from all points of the compass; the flakes of ice, for they were too large to be called hail, came down with such prodigious force as to destroy man and beast; and whoever witnessed that storm, could entertain no doubt of a special providence in the affairs of men. We were all safe moored, and the heart expanded in thankfulness to the Eternal Power that had watched over our safety. Next morning's sun restored the usual Asiatic weather, and a venerable Turk, with a silver beard, very long, was observed pulling from their small settlement with some degree of pomp. On coming up the side, to our great astonishment, he seized the first lieutenant's hand, and in pure English, though with a strong Scottish accent, asked which was Laird Keith. This man, I heard, was of the clan of the Campbells, and had served Djezzar Pacha, the butcher of Syria, who one morning cut off his nose, and banished him from Acre, his capital. He had since risen to the rank of general in the service of the Sublime Porte, and was now sent by the Sultan to concert measures with Lord Keith to expel the French from his Sublime Highness's territory of Egypt. His appearance fully convinced us that parting with the nose did not increase the beauty of the human face divine; but he declared, and we fully believed him, that his old heart warmed at the sight of the tartan that covered some of the military on our deck. Preparations were now made for landing the sick, who in the crowded state of the transports and troop ships were numerous. The pioneers made an open space near the beach, and the sick were encamped under a strong guard, who posted sentinels thickly round the encampment.

The following night was beautifully serene, and the suns of other worlds threw their softened and pensive light on this minute speck in the boundless creation – the watch, some of whom paced the deck, castle-building, and imagining scenes of bliss that never were to be realised, while others admired the starry vault of heaven, wondering with what sort of beings yon myriads of worlds were peopled, while the talkers who could get listeners, were spinning many a long yarn of by-gone days and other scenes. Crombie, a grey-headed young gentleman (for all midshipmen are called *young* gentlemen, and with whom the youthful lieutenant of his watch commonly created some mirth by desiring him as youngster to shin up to the masthead and count the convoy), now seized me by the button, by which he compelled me to listen to his yarn, as follows:– 'I say, youngster, that was an ugly coast we ran down upon yesterday, and reminds me of an occurrence that was particularly mournful' – here he hemmed, and seemed to smother a sigh. 'You see, when I belonged to his Majesty's sloop – but it will be as well not to mention her name, as I cut and run one day without asking permission – well, we were cruising in the latitude, and by Old Soundings' longitude (but that by dead reckoning could not always be depended upon), near where brother Jonathan said he had discovered a dangerous cluster of rocks, to which he had affixed the appropriate name of the "Devil's Grip"; well, I dined in the gunroom that day, and many a hearty laugh at the Yankee notion circulated with the bottle, for the master proved, to the satisfaction of all but one at the table, that rocks could not be in the open sea, so many hundred miles from any known land, and where the deep sea lead could not find bottom, and for which he had often tried in vain; so when the caterer bowed round, to signify that the mess allowance of wine – viz., a pint each person, was drunk, the first luff proposed an extra bottle, while we listened to the most extraordinary youth I ever met with, as he, with fluency of speech and elegance of manner demolished the master's premises and inferences. This young gentleman was called the captain's nephew, and might, I think, have claimed nearer relationship; he was named Paulo, after his mother, Pauline, a Neapolitan countess, who fled from a nunnery, where she had been immured without asking her consent. She must have been a beauty, for her son, though of a very fragile and delicate make, was remarkably tall and handsome, with a most expressive countenance, generally clouded with a shade of melancholy. He was fond of gazing at the moon, and wrote a deal of poetry, comparing ladies' eyes to the bright stars that shone above him, all about love, and such other nonsense; but our doctor, who was a learned man, pronounced it beautiful, and said he was a genius of the first order, full of susceptibility, and with nerves too finely strung for this coarse and bustling world; at all events, he was universally beloved for his gentleness and kindness of heart. At punishment you would see him with his hands clasped, and his eyes suffused with tears, looking up in his uncle's face with such an imploring look to spare the culprit, while the muscles round his well-formed mouth used to work as the sharp lash fell on the tender skin of the sufferer. The captain was a stern, unbending man, but his iron countenance softened at the visible agony of this glorious youth, who frequently gained his point, and the last dozen was remitted. He said, as far as I could understand him, that the shell of the earth was trifling compared to its interior, which was supposed to be in a state of fusion, and hence arose volcanoes and earthquakes, the heaving up of lands that had been the bed of the ocean, and the submersion of others; that the vast Atlantic itself was supposed by some philosopher to have once been habitable, and a great continent. All this was too learned, and made no impression on anyone but the doctor, so we drank the captain's toast, of good afternoon, and went to our usual duty; mine was to keep the first watch. Old Soundings, fortified by a nor'-wester, was officer of the watch. The gale blew hard, right aft, and we were dashing through a heavy sea in merry style. "I think, sir," said I, addressing my officer without touching my hat, the night being too dark for him to notice the omission (a point on which he was very particular), "I think, sir, that the sea seems inclined to kick up a bobbery to-night, and is rising fast." "I am of the same opinion, youngster; but what is that ahead?" At this moment the lookout man on the bowsprit sang out, "Breakers a-head!" and was reiterated by the cat-headmen, "Breakers on both bows!" in that indescribable tone of alarm that carries instant conviction of great danger, and causes a revulsion of the blood. This terrific announcement woke even the sleepers, for in less time than I take to tell you, every man and boy was on deck, most of them in their shirts. Poor dear Paulo, looking more like an aërial sprite than of mortal mould, ran after the captain, who went out on the end of the bowsprit, and looked steadily around, which required nerves of iron, for right ahead seemed a vast barrier of rocks, on which the sea was wildly breaking, throwing its white spray to the clouds, and on each side, as the mad waves receded, were seen their black tops, peeping through the creamy froth that surrounded us; the gallant ship bounding like a greyhound, at the rate of ten knots, full upon them, that would dash her to atoms, for she seemed to me to increase her speed, probably from an indraught in the reef. Then arose the wild shriek of despair from the timid, and stood still the brave; their manly brows blanched, it is true, for it was a sight of such horror, youngster, that my hair turned perfectly white, and I shut my eyes with the sinner's last ejaculation of "God be merciful to me!" but not before I had seen

Paulo – the beautiful and good Paulo – with the scream of a maniac, jump into the boiling surf. The manly tones of the captain's voice were heard high above the breakers, "Port the helm, port – and silence, all of you! your lives depend on your steadiness and prompt obedience. Master, take the weatherwheel, and steer for an opening two points before the starboard-beam; we may find water through the reef where it does not break so heavily – brace forward the yards" – and the lee-gunnel buried itself in the agitated water, as she sprung to the wind. "Let fly the main-top-gallant sheets" – the sail blew to ribbons, and saved the topmast. "Now, master, hard up with the helm, and square away the yards; send her between those high rocks where the sea does not break." The noble ship leaped between them, while the spray from them washed some of the unnerved over the bulwarks, and their last despairing cry was drowned in the roar of the surf. She steered beautifully in the master's able hands, who had frequently declared he could turn her through the eye of a needle, and this channel between the breakers was like one, and very little wider than her mainyard. Nothing was heard from Old Soundings but "Port it is, starboard withal," not forgetting "sir," at the end of each response. As I went to assist him at the wheel, after drawing in a long breath, I heard him mutter, "Who would have thought the Yankee notion true? but it is the Devil's Grip, and a devilish ugly one it is for sartain," "We are through the reef, thank Almighty God!" said the captain; and it came warm from the heart. "Master, we will heave-to till daylight." "Better take a larger offing," said Soundings, "the devil may have a young grip forming in the wake of his mother." "Keep a good look-out for breakers," called the captain; "and Mr. Handsail, shorten sail for laying her to." And we hove-to, a league to leeward of the most frightful cluster of rocks that ever reared their ugly heads above the wide and open sea. "But where is my boy Paulo?" said the captain. I advanced, and gave my doleful story; his strong and pent-up feelings broke down in a torrent of grief, the big tears coursed each other down his weather-beaten cheeks, as he exclaimed, "Oh, Paulo! my good and gentle son, Paulo, would to God that I had died for thee!" There is something so affecting in the grief of a strong mind like the captain's, so firm, that he retained his self-possession in the midst of scenes that paralysed the heart and blenched the boldest front, that all shed tears that heard him exclaim, in the bitter accents of heart-broken misery, that he was bereaved and desolate, and would welcome death as a cessation from intolerable anguish. I alone stood firm, not being of the melt-ing mood, though I dearly loved the boy, who haunts me in my sleep. I saw him last night, plain as I see you, and heard his maniac scream, as he jumped into the agitated waters.'

Saying this, Crombie pulled off my button, and burst into tears. I respected his feelings too much to recall to mind his previous declaration of stoicism. 'The master,' said he, 'called for a nor'-wester to comfort him, saying, "Grief always made him dry."

'The captain did his duty mechanically, but the elasticity of his step, and his manly deportment, had, like his son, left him for ever. He was never after seen to smile, retired on half-pay, and soon went to that bourne from whence no traveller returns.'

Crombie, who under a rough exterior possessed a feeling heart, now paused in his interesting narrative of bygone days, and all on deck that were pacing to and fro stopped short, while every eye was turned on the sick camp, for from that quarter came a shrill and piercing cry, as of human agony in its last extremity, mingled with a complication of roarings and noises that baffles description. Crombie assured me (who was what he called a greenhorn, and Johnny Newcome) that the scream proceeded from an immense number of jackals, and the other noises, that were really deafening, from the wild beasts of the forests, who had been drawn together in masses by the smell of the sick, on whom they must be meditating an attack, and from their cry he supposed them in a voracious state of hunger, and in great force, surrounding three sides of the camp, on which, making use of his expression, they meant to have a 'mortal gorge,' Crombie's favourite term for gluttony. The quick firing of the sentinels, and the sound of the bugle calling the troops to arms, induced Lord Keith to make the night signal for launches manned and armed with carronades, who opened with grape and canister on the forest, and soon drove back the ferocious assailants to their native wilds, while the camp-fire threw its wild glare over the romantic scenery of this little-known but wonderful piece of nature's workmanship on the grandest scale. The next day a greater clearance was effected round the camp, and quantities of fuel brought in to keep large fires burning through the darkness of night; a petty officer and two men were missing at the muster roll, and supposed to have been carried off by the monsters of the woods. Here we lay till the latter end of February, practising our intended operations of landing, repairing damages, and healing the sick, the weather delightful, and plenty of fresh provisions from the Island of Rhodes, to whose governor, the Turkish admiral, acting with us, ordered a bastinado on the soles of the feet for some deficiency in the supply, and it proved a very effective mode. On the 28th of February, we saw the low, sandy coast of Egypt, or rather Pompey's Pillar, near Alexandria, received the report of the blockading squadron, and anchored in Aboukir Bay on the 1st of March; unfortunately the weather came on so bad as to occasion a heavy surf on the beach, the intended scene of our operations. During the gale the *Foudroyant* struck heavily on the wreck of the *Orient*, the ship of the unfortunate Bruyes, who was burnt in that celebrated action that so deservedly immortalised the name of Nelson.

LANDING OF THE BRITISH ARMY IN EGYPT

On the 8th of March 1801, at nine in the morning, all the boats of the British fleet under Vice-Admiral Lord Keith were assembled in a triple line, extending about a mile and a half, at a league distance from their intended place of debarkation, being that part of the sandy shore of Africa called Egypt, and in the Bay of Aboukir, or shoals near to the place celebrated for giving birth to Cleopatra. The centre line, composed of flats and launches, were crowded to excess with the flower of the British army. These were towed by barges and pinnaces, while a line of jolly-boats and cutters moved in the rear, to assist the disabled. They were drawn up with beautiful precision, the captains of divisions in front, while the Hon. A. Cochrane, who commanded, was considerably in advance with St. George's flag displayed. His barge led the whole of the triple lines. Opposite, and immediately in front, lay the French army on sandhills, whose ridges were strongly fortified with heavy pieces of ordnance, while here and there, between the hills, peeped out the flying artillery; and the cavalry showed in numbers between the masses of infantry, that looked sufficiently numerous to devour our small but heroic band. On their left lay Aboukir (now Nelson's) Island, strongly fortified with mortars. The scene was beautiful and imposing, the line-of-battle ships in the distant perspective, with the bombs, sloops, and troopships in shore. The sun shone with great splendour, and its fierce rays shot down on our troops with intense heat. The light breeze, that gently rippled the placid waters, was just sufficient to gaily waft the various flags and colours that decorated and distinguished our different divisions, while the heavy Crescent of the Turks lay dormant to its staff.

The signal is thrown out to advance leisurely, but to keep strictly in line till under fire, and then use every exertion to land the troops. Fountain of mercy and love! that this splendid and bright scene of nature's sublimity should be marred and totally defaced by man! What answer shall be given to the question of the Eternal, 'Man, why sheddest thou thy brother's blood?' Alas, alas! the wholesale slaughter of that day! all that military skill could effect in making the intended place of our debarkation invulnerable had been done by the French governor of Alexandria; and for eight days had we, by our presence in this bay, given him due notice of our intention. To his commander-in-chief, General Menou, he wrote, 'that nothing with life could be thrown on his shores but a cat'; in fact, he had rendered the beach impregnable; and so it was to all but the steady valour of British bands. Imagine, fair reader (if any of the loveliest part of God's creation honour me so far), imagine ten thousand of England's hardy sons, full of life and vigour, rushing into an unequal contest that, in the space of one hour, would decimate them. Hark! the first shell from Nelson's Island; the roar, the whistle, and explosion among the boats, answered by the heart-stirring cheers of the British lines. The heavy artillery from the ridge of sandhills in front open their iron throats on the devoted boats. 'Give way fore and aft!' is the respondent cry to the shrieks of the wounded, the heavy groans of the dying, and the gurgling sounds of the drowning. Gaps are seen in our line, and the brave soldier struggling in the water, encumbered by his accoutrements; his ammunition, his three days' provision and water, give him no chance of floating till the light boats can grasp him. Now their flying artillery, with their long train of horses, gallop to the beach, and open their brazen mouths on our still advancing boats. That most venerable and veteran son of war, Sir Ralph Abercrombie, commander-in-chief, in the *Kent*'s barge, moving in the rear, now desired the officer of that boat to pass through the gaps in our line, and place him in front of the fire. 'I command you, sir,' said the veteran; 'my personal safety is nothing compared with the national disgrace of the boats turning back. Example is needful in this tremendous fire, which exceeds all I ever saw. O God! they waver – onward, brave Britons, onward!' This apparent wavering was occasioned by a shell sinking the *Foudroyant's* flat boat with sixty soldiers in her, and by the rush of smaller ones to pick up the sinking soldiery. The lieutenant in command of the barge respectfully said, he had the orders of Sir Richard Bickerton, not to expose the general-in-chief unnecessarily to fire, or land him till the second division were on shore. The British lines, closing, to cover their heavy losses, rapidly approached the landing-place. The French infantry in heavy masses now lined the beach, and the roar of musketry was incessant and tremendous. Sir Ralph, in great agitation, again ordered the officer to put his boat in front of the triple line, and was met by that officer respectfully declaring that 'he would obey the orders of his admiral alone.' The old General made an abortive attempt to jump overboard, saying, 'Without some striking example, human nature could not face such fire'; and, indeed, the sea was ploughed and strongly agitated by the innumerable balls that splashed among the boats, sometimes hiding them altogether by the spray they created. This was a most painful scene for a spectator: our friends mowed down like corn before the reaper. But now a change comes over it. A heart-stirring cheer is given on the prows touching the beach: the soldiers, heartily tired of being shot at like rooks, spring from the boats with great alacrity; that effective instrument, the bayonet, is actively at work on both sides. Our brave soldiers in landing jumped on the French muskets, for the beach was firmly disputed, but the home thrusts of the nervous British arm, and their dauntless hearts, drove back the Frenchmen, who, in regaining their first position, opened for their cavalry to charge our line, then forming, and for the first time that day with loaded muskets. It was an anxious moment for us, who were spectators, to see the fleet Arabian horses moving in a whirlwind of sand, upon our half-formed regiments. Onward they came, like the lightning's flash. 'Sare,' said Lord Keith (in his own broad Scottish accent) to the artillery officer of the bombship he was in, lying as close in shore as the shoal water would permit, 'geeve those incarnate deevils ane o' your largest shells.' The explosion, in sweeping the French commanding officer and numerous others to their great account, caused a halt and partial confusion amongst them. The cool and determined front presented by the Forty-second might, in some measure, have created delay in their furious charge. The majority drew up, and the well-directed volley of the second and third ranks of our line over the front one, kneeling to receive the horses of the enemy on their bayonets, made them wheel about and retrograde in quick time, while about sixty furiously and rashly rode in on our troops. Man and horse disappeared in the twinkling of an eye, and the whole line heard the cheering orders, 'Charge bayonets; advance in the double quick time!'

These were received with the truly British shout that no nation can equal, the determined valour it expresses carrying dismay to the opposing force. I saw the British commanding officer, Sir John Moore, in front, waving his men onward with his hat. Up the sandhills they rushed, appearing to me like a heavy wave rolling up a sandy beach. The French forces were astounded, dismayed, and disheartened; and their want of that steady, persevering, and indomitable spirit, that nerves the brave man to encounter misfortune to the last, was now observable in their retreat. They left some of their field-pieces in our hands, which proved most valuable, as they served to freshen up and accelerate the speed of their rearguard. Our forces took possession of their first line of defence, and bivouacked on it for the night. In no action during this eventful war of a quarter of a century, did the fine qualities of our soldiers and sailors display themselves in brighter colours than during the landing in Egypt, on the 8th of March 1801.

ALARM

'What are the drums beating to quarters for?' called the reefers, as they hastily ascended the cockpit ladder of the *Foudroyant*.

'Have you not heard,' said a wag, the wit of the lower regions, 'that Menou is swimming off, at the head of his army, to take our flagship by escalade?'

'But what has he done with Sir Ralph and his army?'

'Ate them for breakfast before starting.'

But this badinage was woefully changed when the loblolly boy, looking like Shakespeare's starved apothecary, whispered, in solemn tones, 'The ship is on fire in the gunner's storeroom!'

And as the said storeroom was not very remote from the grand magazine, the information created anything but pleasurable feelings. As each fell into the station assigned to him in battle, a feverish state of nervous twitchings might be discerned by the curious observer. My place on the poop in the signal department fully displayed before me the conduct of my superiors, commonly called by reefers the 'big-wigs.' Captain Philip Beaver,[2] commanding the ship, was cool, collected and active. 'Let the boarders assist the firemen in handing the water below,' called he, through his trumpet; 'and every other man and officer remain at his quarters on pain of death. Officers of the guard, post detachments of marines on the quarterdeck, forecastle, and poop, load their muskets with ball, and fire on any person, whatever his rank may be, who endeavours to quit the ship without orders.'

This, said in a stern, commanding tone, withdrew the wandering glances I, with many others, cast at the placid waters around us; for the idea of standing over gunpowder enough to blow twenty such ships into myriads of atoms, was far from agreeable. Lord Keith looked pale, and stood without his hat; his feelings, from the recent loss of the *Queen Charlotte*, must have been acute. I saw the smoke rising from the fore-hatchway, and every now and then, from the strength of imagination *alone*, thought I felt the ship lifting under me. 'We will have the signal of distress ready, and also for all the boats in the fleet to assemble round the flagship, Thompson,' said I, addressing my brother signal-midshipman.

'Right, my boy; and we will take our stand here, where we can easily jump overboard, if we find the grand magazine sending us star-gazing. Were you ever half-drowned?'

'A little experience that way,' said I.

'Now listen to my short yarn, while you keep a sharp eye on the fore-hatchway. Just previous to leaving school, I went to bathe with

[2] Captain Philip Beaver was a distinguished officer, whose premature death alone prevented his rising to high rank in the navy. He served in the action between Keppel and d'Orvilliers, off Ushant, July 1778, and in Rodney's action off St. Lucia with De Guichen in 1780. As Captain of the *Foudroyant*, flagship of Lord Keith, he directed the bombardment of Genoa in 1800 assisted at the landing of the troops in Aboukir Bay, 1801, and at Martinique in 1809. He was Commodore at the capture of the *Isle of France* in 1810, was present at the capture of Java in 1811, and died at the Cape, in command of the *Nisus*, 5th April 1813.

a favourite schoolfellow in a pit whose bottom was composed of white sand, and about twelve or thirteen feet deep. Jacques was the first undressed, and sprang a good distance into the pit: all at once I heard his agonised cry of distress; and, with my lower garments on, rushed to his assistance. He seemed to me cramped, and unable to struggle; his head and one hand alone above the water – that hand extended towards me, and his eyes, with the imploring look of despair, bent upon me. At once it rushed across my mind – may God forgive my cowardice and selfishness – that his clutch would drag me down with him. I hesitated, halted, and kept out of his grasp, while the poor youth was gradually sinking; but when the water reached his mouth, the impeded respiration forced the blood upwards and crimsoned his pale forehead; his orbs of sight, that seemed starting from strangulation, assumed a reproachful look of intense agony; – the waters closed over his innocent head, while I, who could have saved him, looked on paralysed – no other hand was near but mine, and that was nerveless! O God! my feelings of horror, fear, and shame, you may imagine, but I cannot depict them. I called with all my power for help – alas! none came. I swam into the circle caused by his sinking – I looked down, for the white sand gave a clearness to the water, and, oh, merciful God! I saw his right hand extend itself to reach my feet, his head thrown back, and the same despairing, reproachful look that will ever remain fixed in my heart and mind while memory retains her seat. I was mad with terror, and remained spellbound to the spot where the unfortunate Jacques lay beneath me, his right hand still extended, with the fingers clutched on its palm. He moved one of his legs with a convulsive motion, and half raised his body to a sitting posture. It was the last expiring effort of nature – he fell on his back, and remained motionless. I see by your averted looks that you hate me, but your hate cannot exceed my own. I have only to plead my youth and a constitutional timidity, owing, I think, to excessive foresight or anticipation. You perceive my nerves are as firmly strung at this moment of peril as your own, and I am confident I can meet danger and death with unshrinking fortitude; but I have a hesitation of incurring that peril; and, as my father truly observed on the melancholy death of my friend Jacques, I am one more inclined to act with prudence than rash courage, which, in a sarcastic way, he denominated the better part of valour.'

At this moment one of the junior officers came hastily up the quarter-deck ladder, calling to Captain Beaver not to be frightened, as the fire was got under.

'Pray, sir,' said our gallant captain, 'what sort of a sensation is fear? I know it not, but I see how it looks. Beat the retreat, and pipe to dinner.'

THE DEATH OF ABERCROMBIE

On the 20th of March, a Bedouin Arab sought Sir Sidney Smith in the British camp, established before Alexandria. These Arabs (who are the robbers of the desert) came into the camp every morning thousands strong, forming a daily market of mutton, fowl, buffalo beef, and vegetables, which, under excellent regulations, were sold at a very reasonable rate. Their appearance was wild and interesting, and the son frequently led the ass that conveyed his blind father, numbers having lost their sight from the 'ophthalmia,' that dreadful scourge of the Egyptian shore. The Arab's information was important. He was sent by his chief to say that a large reinforcement of Frenchmen, with the commander-in-chief, Menou, had been tracked and harassed by his band from Grand Cairo to Alexandria, into which place they had thrown themselves last night. On this important information, the order of the day commanded the assembling of the troops two hours before the usual time (which had hitherto been daylight).

On the following morning, the men were mustering in the trenches and batteries, when the videttes rode in at a furious rate, their horses covered with foam. Their information convinced us of the discernment of Sir Sidney Smith in anticipating the measures of the foe. A numerous French army were advancing rapidly against us, stealing upon us in the darkness of the night. In came our advanced posts, who had been ordered to retire on the main body if overpowered. This was now the case, and they stated the advancing enemy to be in great force, and in a most excited state, from the quantity of brandy that must have been administered to them before they left Alexandria. Now the heavy and measured tread of the masses of infantry broke on the silence of the stilly night, while the neighing and prancing of the warhorse gave intimation of the cavalry being in great force on each flank of the advancing army. The stillness of death prevailed in our camp, save and except the dashing of the aides-de-camp in front of the line as they flew with the orders of the general-in-chief to the different batteries not to throw away their fire, but reserve the grape and canister till the enemy touched the muzzles of the guns. As our troops closed their files with bayonets glittering, which might be distinguished by the watch-fires that threw a lurid glare over our well-formed line, showing the firm determination of the troops by their compressed lips and the nervous grasp by which they held their muskets; their long and hard drawn breath, the left foot slightly advanced, and the whole carriage betokening a firm determination to do or die, convinced the observing that their nerves were well braced to the coming deadly encounter. 'Silence, and steady, men,' were the words of command heard along the line. The French trumpets sounded a charge, and everything was in wild commotion.

The British cheer rang high above the sharp volleys of musketry, the batteries threw in their death-dealing round, but the French army advanced in rapid style, overthrowing all before them, till the British bayonet transfixed their front rank; even that did not force them back. The survivors rushed on, and when day broke never were hostile armies more intermingled; here a Frenchman and there an Englishman. Now came the deadly strife of man to man; and the brave veteran who commanded in chief (he was upwards of sixty!) was engaged hand to hand with a young French dragoon, and would have fallen under the weight of his sabre cuts, had not a friendly bayonet lifted the man out of his saddle, leaving his sword entangled in Sir Ralph's clothes. The gallant veteran seized the sword, and shortly afterwards was shot close up to the hip joint, by a musket ball lodging in the bone. The anguish must have been acute; but no symptoms, not even a groan, made known that he was suffering. When obliged to acknowledge himself wounded, he called it slight, and refused to retire to the rear.

The Hon. Captain Proby, now addressing the commander-in-chief, to whom he was aide-de-camp, reported the enemy to be retreating, covered by their cavalry. 'But good God, General, you are seriously wounded, your saddle is saturated with blood. Let me support you to the rear, and for all our sakes let the surgeons examine you.'

'Captain Proby, I thank you,' said the veteran, with a faint voice; 'but in these stirring times the General should be the last person to think of self. Captain Proby, order a forward movement, and hang fiercely on the retiring foe. Desire Hompesh's dragoons to cut through their rear-guard, and follow them closely to the walls of Alexandria.' Seeing hesitation and great concern in the ingenuous, youthful countenance of Captain Proby, Sir Ralph added with sternness, 'See my orders instantly obeyed, sir.'

And the aide-de-camp, dashing his spurs into the flank of the swift Arabian, flew along the line, vociferating the orders of 'Forward! forward!' at the same time despatching the first dragoon he met with to Colonel Abercrombie, stating his opinion that his father was bleeding to death on the field with a gunshot wound. Sir Ralph, seeing Sir Sidney Smith's horse shot under him, now desired his orderly to remount him. Sir Sidney, thinking it would inconvenience the General, refused to mount, till a ball from their retreating artillery decided the question by killing the orderly. While Sir Sidney (who was wounded) was thanking the General, Colonel Abercrombie galloped up – 'Dear father, has your wound been examined?'

Sir Ralph, who was sinking fast from loss of blood, now turned affectionately to the manly form of his son, who stood at his side in a visible agony of suspense, muttered the words – 'A flesh wound – a mere scratch!' and fell fainting into his arms.

He was quickly borne by orderly sergeants to the rear, where the wound was pronounced of a dangerous nature. Fortunately the *Foundroyant's* launch had just reached the beach with boats of the fleet to convey the wounded off to the shipping; and the hero of sixty-three, in an insensible state, was consigned to the tender care of his son, exposed to the fierce sun, whose rays shot down hot enough to melt him. Colonel Abercrombie held one of his hands, while tender commiseration clouded his manly brow. I saw this gallant and good old warrior extended on a grating, coming along-side the flagship, his silvery hair streaming in the breeze that gently rippled the waters – his venerable features convulsed with agony, while the sun darted fiercely on him its intense rays, combining with his wound to occasion the perspiration to pour down his fore-head like heavy drops of rain; yet he commanded not only his groans, but even his sighs, lest they should add to the evident anguish depicted in Colonel Abercrombie's countenance, as he wiped the perspiration from his father's face.

'We are near the *Foudroyant*, my dear sir; swallow a little of the contents of my canteen, it will enable you better to bear the motion of being hoisted in.'

'Send the quarter-masters below to sling the General,' said Lord Keith; 'and select careful hands to the whip,' and his lordship's countenance expressed the deepest commiseration. 'Now, whip handsomely – bear off the side, gentlemen – for God's sake do not let the grating come in contact with anything. High enough – lower handsomely – see that the bearers are equally tall. Now rest the grating gently on their shoulders;' and his lordship gazed on the suffering countenance of the ancient soldier.

'I am putting you to great inconvenience,' said Sir Ralph; and added, in faltering accents, 'I am afraid I shall occasion you much more trouble.'

'The greatest trouble, General,' and Lord Keith took hold of one of the wounded man's hands, 'is to see you in this pitiable situation.'

Lord Keith pressed, relinquished the hand, and burst into tears; nor was there a dry eye that witnessed the sufferings of this venerated and venerable warrior. He lingered in acute pain three days, and his body was sent down to Malta. He was father to the late learned Speaker of the House of Commons, and as a man or a soldier was never excelled. Peace to his *manes*!

GUNBOAT ATTACK IN 1805

'We will play Old Snuffy[3] a trick this evening,' said my very youthful commander (for I do not think he had numbered sixteen years) to me, as, in company with the squadron, we were standing in for the Spanish Main under the command of the respectable commodore, designated by my captain as Old Snuffy.

'In what way, sir?' replied I.

'Why, as soon as the sun goes down, up stick and make all sail for the Gulf of Mexico, where we are sure to make our fortunes.'

This was a clincher, and no person disputed the propriety of such conduct, which was pursued to the very letter, as his Majesty's sloop *Elk* made the town of Carthagena on the succeeding evening.

[3] Lieut. J. R. Dacres, son of Vice-Admiral J. R. Dacres, at that time Commander-in-Chief on the Jamaica station.

'Hoist the yawl and gig out, and select your men and officers,' said my commander; 'and pick up all you can, for we are not known to be on the coast.'

'Had we not better anchor the sloop with a spring on her cable, first?'

'No, no; be off, and leave her to me.'

And we did leave her, as commanded, to pull round Bird Island, and into the Boccachica. We were all strangers to the West Indies, having shortly before arrived from England.

'Jack Whitewood,' said I to the master, 'pull foot for yonder lateen-rigged boat, and bring her down to me, the commodore. What is her cargo?'

'Melons and pumpkins.'

'Select a supply of the best melons for the boats, and let her go anywhere but to Carthagena.'

And we lay on the oars, and indulged in a mortal gorge on melons, letting the boat drift at the caprice of the currents. This was employment very passable in a West India night, and served to while away the lingering hours of darkness. As day began to dawn, we gave chase to eleven large lateen-rigged boats; but observing they appeared warlike, and made no show of avoiding us, I called the gig alongside, and lay upon our oars.

'Let us wait for broad daylight, Jack Whitewood, they may be gunboats, and we shall have caught a Tartar, instead of making our fortunes. There is up square sail, and out sweeps, by Jupiter! They are what I suspected, and full of men, with a long gun in their bow. Now, boys, stretch to your oars; for, if taken, into the mines they will pop us. Coxswain, steer close in with Bird Island, and look out for sunken rocks.'

The coxswain, whose name was Burroughs, had narrowly escaped the fate of Parker and other active mutineers in '98. He was a good seaman, a high-spirited ruffian, and filled the situation of boatswain's mate in the sloop with credit to himself; but he was a complete daredevil, and a dangerous man. 'Sir,' said he, addressing me respectfully, 'the gunboats are gaining rapidly on us, for the breeze has freshened, and they will speedily open their fire. I would advise you to land on Bird Island, destroy the boats, and cross to the side, where the brig will see our signals and take us on board.'

'Very good,' whispered the talkative midshipman by my side, who had been entertaining me with a glowing account of the mines of Potosi, and the pleasure we should experience in digging up gold and silver for others during the remainder of our lives. 'A capital idea!' said he; 'and I trust, sir, you will act upon it.'

'And get murdered by him for so acting,' replied I. 'The devil-may-care boy would desire no better sport than to prey on Carthagena as captain of such a gang, well armed as they are. Now, observe how the villain is edging her in shore. Gig ahoy! Jack Whitewood, speed for the brig, and bring her down to our assistance.'

'Ay, ay, sir; though truly sorry to leave you in such a slow coach to experience the tender mercy of these guarda-costas. They will put you into the mines, never to see the light of the sun again.'

'Lads, you hear what Mr. Whitewood says, and it is true. If our officers, who are very young, covet such a situation, we shall be great fools to allow them to sacrifice us.'

During this mutinous speech I had been working up my nerves for a deed of horror – to shoot the coxswain through the head. Burroughs looked around to mark the impression made by his speech on the men. During this time I had worked my resolution up to the sad necessity of imbruing my hands in human blood, as an act of self-preservation, and of duty to my country. Drawing a loaded pistol from my breast, and placing it to his head, 'Another word, Burroughs, and you are a dead man. Obey my orders instantly, and in silence; take the stroke oar.' The ruffian rolled his fierce eyes over me. He saw determination in my looks, and heard it in my voice. The clink of cocking the pistol had evidently not escaped his notice or hearing, and the expression of his eyes plainly said, 'If I give this striping as food for the fish, will the crew join me or surrender me up to justice?' I watched every motion with intense anxiety, and whispered to the gallant and loquacious youngster, now a post captain, to fire on any one of the crew that rose to succour Burroughs. He reluctantly and slowly lowered his murderous gaze, and took the stroke oar.

'Now, Thompson,' calling to the man he had relieved, 'take the helm, and keep her close in shore, with a good look-out for sunken rocks. Throw everything out of the boat but your arms, tear up the bottom boards, and lighten her in every way. Now put your trust in

God, and give way; and, with coolness and resolution, I have little doubt but we shall escape the dreaded mines of Potosi; at all events, we will sell our liberty dearly. Give way fore and aft, and mind your steerage.'

At this moment the foremost gunboat loaded and ran forward her long gun, which they trained and pointed on the yawl. Our muskets were ranged in the stern-sheets; and the sitters, consisting of the officers and two marines, now threw a glance on the foremost foe, and gazed on each other, awaiting, with all the patience they could muster, the effect of the round and grape momentarily expected. 'By God! she is on the rocks,' said Burroughs, breaking his moody and sullen silence. She was, and over on her beam ends. I breathed more freely on observing the second boat stopping to assist her consort; and after a heavy pull against the current, we got on board the brig. To the joint advice of the master and myself, to take an offing for fear of a night attack from such a formidable force, his reply was, that if they dared to attack his Majesty's sloop under his command, he would blow them into a place not to be named to ears polite. As this, in some measure, conveyed a reproof, we made our bow, and retired to our cabins to obtain some repose, of which we all stood in need.

'Sir, coffee is ready,' said my servant, waking me out of a profound nap.

'Coffee before quarters?' replied I.

'No,' said my youthful captain, 'I would not allow those who appeared so fatigued to be disturbed; and the second luff and I have put the brig in order to receive your friends, who were so desirous of your company this morning, if they dare presume to attack us.'

Saying this, my youthful commander seated himself at our table.

The heavy report of a gun, the whistle, a crash, the death groan of Richard Bennet, our senior mate, and the agonised shriek of our steward, Saunders Lackey, whose legs were shot off, were all heard the next instant. The cabin boy had likewise his arm broken by this most disastrous shot, whose effects, from its suddenness, seemed to have paralysed us. 'Pipe to quarters!' shouted I, and rushed upon deck, closely followed by all that were able from the cabin. Here I found darkness and confusion. The men, alarmed at the rushing of the water into the sloop (for the shot had hit us below the watermark) now stood huddled together. 'To your quarters,' cried I, 'and cast loose your guns. Can any person make out the gunboats?'

'Here is the spy-glass,' said the youngster of the watch, with which I swept the horizon.

'There they are,' said I to the captain, 'eleven in number, pulling up in three divisions on our larboard quarter. Break off the after guns, and haul upon the starboard spring – veer away cable!'

'The spring has slipped up to the bows,' called the second luff, from the forecastle.

'This was bent by a lubber,' said I to my commander. 'We must cut from the anchor, sir, and get on the sweeps.'

'Do as you think best,' was the reply; and we accordingly cut, and with the sweeps kept her head seaward. Burroughs, with great activity and courage, got out two long guns aft, and commenced firing on the gunboats, which by this time were close on our stern and quarters, keeping up an incessant fire from their bow-guns and musketry, and with great yelling and shouting evinced a disposition to board.

At this moment, Mr. Mather, the boatswain, an Irishman, above six feet in height, and well-proportioned, came aft to me, and, pulling off his hat, with the greatest coolness, said, 'By Jasus, sir, these wild devils will be on board us, if you do not check them by a broadside.'

The advice was sound, and the mode of delivery, at such an exciting time, unique. This excellent warrant-officer, when he heard our youthful commander read his commission, opened his goggle eyes to a larger extent than usual, and with an inimitably ludicrous smile, asked me if it was not a joke; but when assured by me that it was downright earnest, slapped his thigh, and in a strong Hibernian accent said, 'That bates Bannagher.'

'Lay the sweeps athwart, and load the larboard guns with grape and canister – hard a-starboard the helm, and fire as you bring them to bear, taking great care not to waste your shot.'

The sweeps, that had only given us steerage-way, thus enabled us to bring our larboard broadside full upon them, and the eighteen-pound carronades, from the crowded state of the boats, did infinite execution, and put a stop to their yells, shouting, and disposition to board. They immediately retrograded, and left us without further molestation.

Having got sail on the brig – for a light breeze had sprung up – I went below to contemplate a most melancholy sight, the mutilated remains of our steward and Richard Bennet. Here was my young commander, weeping bitterly over the bodies, and accusing himself as the cause of their destruction. Lackey's legs were shot off close up to the hips; and as the surgeon (who was a Scotchman) was attempting to get tourniquets on the stumps, the poor wounded Highlander, with that strong love for country that so exalts them, dwelt entirely on his far-distant home. 'O Scotland!' said he, kissing the doctor's hand, 'I thought I should never see your bonny hills again.'

But Bennet – poor Richard Bennet! – it was only the day previous to sailing from Port Royal that he came to me the very personification of perfect happiness. The cause was a letter from the commander-in-chief's secretary, promising him the first vacancy. 'Oh, the exquisite pleasure the knowledge of this will give to thee, thou matchless piece of nature's workmanship!' apostrophising a miniature that he rapturously kissed.

'Will you let me see it, Bennet?' And he presented me with the likeness of a beautiful girl of eighteen, on whose alabaster and polished brow modesty sat enthroned, while her celestial blue eyes gave indication of a warm, affectionate heart, governed by a well-regulated mind; but I can feel the effect of female loveliness more vividly than I can describe it. 'She is all that youthful poets fancy when they love,' observed I, 'and you are a most fortunate youth in possessing Heaven's best gift, a virtuous female's heart.'

'Oh, sir, did you know that heart! – it is the seat of every good feeling. My blessed Susette!' And again he rapturously pressed the picture to his lips, while his heart beat wildly as he replaced the miniature on it.

I thought of these things, and turned away much depressed, taking the miniature and a lock of the brown tresses that clustered round his handsome forehead, mentally vowing to place them in Susette's possession the first opportunity; and I kept that vow, and found a dying angel, looking more ethereal than mortal. It was at the close of day, when a bright July sun was on the point of setting, that I arrived at the very pretty cottage of Susette's mother. I tremulously stated who I was to the most respectable looking matron I ever saw, of French extraction. In broken and bitter accents of heartfelt grief, she told me her daughter's death was daily looked for, and requested time to prepare her to see me. At last she expressed a wish to see the friend of Richard Bennet, and I was admitted to the fairest daughter of Eve that ever found this rugged world ungenial to its tender blossoms. She was propped up with pillows near the open lattice of her bedroom, that was clustered with roses. Her white dress and the drapery of the room accorded with the angelic vision who now turned her lustrous orbs upon me. They would have been too dazzling, had not bountiful nature, in pity to man, veiled them in long-fringed eyelids. She held out her transparent hand, and gently pressed mine as I knelt to kiss it; and as she felt my tears drop on it, softly murmured, 'I wish I could cry – it would relieve my poor heart!' She gasped for breath, and respired with great difficulty. 'The lock of hair – quickly, while I can see it!' She caught at it, wildly pressed it to her lips and heart, and fell back. Her mother and I thought she had fainted, but her pure and innocent soul had returned to the God that gave it.

THE YOUTHFUL COMMANDER'S CRUISE

The bodies of the slain were committed to the deep the following morning with due solemnity and sincere grief, particularly from my youthful captain, who abstained from his favourite pastime of hopscotch that evening. 'Who is for hopscotch?' said our noble commander, of an evening, directing his question to his officers in the gunroom. The usual exclamation of 'The devil!' and a stare at each other, was our mode of receiving this out-of-the-way invitation. 'Jack Whitewood,' said our commander, 'will you not take a hop?' Jack gave his lengthened visage a most inimitable twist, as he discarded his old quid in favour of a larger; and with an aside that beats cock-fighting, answered loudly, 'Ay, ay, sir!' at the same time putting the best foot (for one of them was defective), for the purpose of kicking a bung about in certain squares, bearing the names of Little Jack, Big Belly, etc. etc. These innocent amusements and officer-like recreations, though they enabled Jack Whitewood to kick himself into a better berth, did not tend to preserve discipline. This is not a solitary instance, in the good old times, of boys being appointed to command men. I remember a marine officer, when the president of a court-martial told him, in most impressive terms, 'that the sentence of this court is, that you shall be deprived of your commission, and never serve His Majesty, his heirs, or successors,' took snuff with the greatest nonchalance, and jocularly asked one of his judges what his age might be that day. The captain, who was one of the many ornaments of the service, and subsequently, and deservedly, reached the highest grade in his profession, declined answering the *broken* officer's question. 'It matters not,' said the prisoner. 'Mr. President, and gentlemen of this honourable court, your sentence is not worth the pinch of snuff I am taking – one of my judges is under age!' If *not dead*, he is still on the marine list.

We cruised and toiled, day and night, but caught no fish, though once we threw away a most excellent chance. A small American ship, at the close of day, who had not led us a dance in chase, hove-to, in very polite style, to receive our boarding officer; and was much praised for his civility in allowing us, without squabbling, to impress two of his prime seamen, which (*entre nous*) my youthful commander was fond of doing. In consequence of this kindness, and presents well applied, the search on board was not rigorous, and the show of each other's colours said good-bye in a most friendly manner. Forty-eight hours after parting company, the impressed men stated that she had loaded with money in Vera Cruz for Havanna; and although we used our best endeavours to anticipate her off her port, we did not succeed, but bought some useful experience, always to distrust Yankee politeness.

As water began to run short, after an ineffectual attempt to find some at the dry Tortugas, we stood for the Spanish Main, and anchored in Honda Bay. The casique, or chief Indian of the place, honoured us with a visit, and brought his daughter, attended with some state. She had a perfect figure, eyes like diamonds, long black tresses, white teeth, and would have passed for a handsome brunette, had she been accustomed to soap, water, and brushes; but these, I believe, had not been introduced into his majesty's dominions, for he termed himself king, and brother of George of England, to whose health he so often drank out of the neck of a bottle of rum, as to get gloriously intoxicated. He was the strongest man I ever saw, to judge from his muscles and breadth of shoulders, which exceeded all the men I had seen; and to give us an opinion of his power, he discharged an arrow into the shoulder of one of his attendants when on shore, who ran off into the woods with great yelling. But in spite of the savage state in which she had been reared, the princess had her maiden modesty and the softness of her gentle sex about her; nor did she take any of the intoxicating draughts which made her father so furious, but did all in her power to check his mad career. Even in that state, the feelings that elevate the human creation above the brute, is most strikingly developed in woman; who –

'In our hours of ease,
Uncertain, coy, and hard to please;
When pain and anguish wring the brow,
A ministering angel thou.'

Finding water difficult to obtain, we up anchor, and stood along the Spanish Main in search of a bay, under the heights of Santa Martha, in which a frigate of ours had procured water, after a desperate fight with ourang-outangs, or man monkeys; at least, so the captain of the frigate reported at Jamaica; and early one fine morning we made the said heights. The tops of the mountains, eternally clad in snow, looked like white clouds far as the sight could reach, and deceived us so much in distance, that the gig, with Jack Whitewood, was sent to sound the bay, thinking it about two leagues off, when they proved it to be six or seven. Anchored close in with the beach at the mouth of a small river, into which we conveyed all our empty casks, and most of the crew of the brig were employed in watering. Having the command of the party, I posted sentinels close on each bank of the rivulet, for the underwood was too thick to allow us to penetrate the immense forests; but the greatest enemy I found, was the sand-fly, which drew blood every bite, and caused great irritation and pain. On mustering at quarters in the evening, I found eight men missing who had been of the watering party, of whom we never heard afterwards. Guns were fired at intervals in the night, and a false alarm of gunboats broke in upon our rest. My young captain informed me that he had a presentiment that he should be killed this cruise, and in that case he had so arranged that I should be made a commander into the sloop; but he was a false prophet, and no such luck ever fell to my lot. At daylight, took a drum and party on shore to search for our lost comrades; but a Spanish schooner led us in chase off the coast, and it took three weeks to beat back again; but this being, like most cruises, dry and uninteresting, except to those concerned, I will bring His Majesty's sloop to an anchor at Port Royal, without having made our fortunes, or, indeed, bettered them in the smallest degree. My youthful commander was thanked in public orders for his skill and bravery in the gunboat attack, made a post-captain, and I was sent home second lieutenant of the convoy ship, to be paid off on my arrival, and to seek out the heart-broken Susette.

THE SINKING SHIP

At the beginning of November, in the year 1807, His Majesty's line-of-battle-ship *Orion* was detached from the squadron in Basque Roads, commanded by Sir Harry Burrard Neale, for the purpose of procuring water at the Glennan Rocks, a very strange cluster of both high and sunken ones, lying off L'Orient. On one of the highest stands a fort, well protected from British assault by its intricate and rocky situation. The November sun, on the Sabbath morning on which His Majesty's ship was running most carelessly off the wind, with the top-gallant sails and foresail set, almost rivalled a splendid June's; and as the noble warlike fabric moved gracefully over the waters amid this dangerous cluster of rocks, at the rate of five miles an hour, every heart seemed elated, and every eye beamed with pleasure, for indeed the day was most joyous, and, for the time of year, uncommon. In a moment, and without warning, I, with the rest on the quarter-deck, was prostrated, and heard the solid oak rent and torn by the harder rock, on which she ran with her bows high in air, while her stern in proportion was depressed – it must have been pointed like a steeple, for this vast body sallied over, and shipped an immense quantity of water through the lower deck ports. The shout of surprise and horror from six hundred men, with the universal cry of 'Lower down the ports!' was astounding. 'Throw all a-back!' called the captain, 'and signalise Sir George Collier that he is standing into danger!'

'He has anchored, sir, with the same signal to us flying at his masthead.'

Our captain looked much agitated, and I thought his commission not worth a straw; for we had come into this dangerous predicament without a pilot, or any precaution by chart or look-

out; and God knows, our situation could not be worse; sticking on
a rock that had already sent alongside forty feet of our keel, in the
bottom of the Bay of Biscay, and in sight of an enemy's squadron
in L'Orient, who now, by bending sails, evinced a disposition to
finish us. The rush of water into the ship was plainly heard from
the lower deck, as I, by the order of the captain, transported the
foremost guns aft, the tide being then flowing. 'I have sent for
you,' said my captain, with solemnity, 'to give you the same
chance as others. The ship will float off into deep water
immediately; but how long she may remain buoyant on that
water, God only knows; from the carpenter's report, I dread the
worst. Cheer them up at the pumps.'

Now she rose, and all sail was made, standing out on the reverse
course that we had entered.

'Telegraph Sir George Collier to keep his frigate as near us as
possible, as we are in a state of great distress, and making more
water than I choose shall be known.' And both ships cleared the
Glennan Rocks, and bore up for Plymouth, with a favourable light
breeze, all the pumps going. At six p.m. the men were placed in
three watches, and one watch ordered to get their suppers and two
hours' sleep, in the best way they could, by planking it on the wet
deck. At nine, the captain gave an order that the officers of the
middle watch should turn in, and down I went, from a very dark
night and a murky sky – the water in the vessel rather on the
increase – and in two minutes was asleep in my cot, having used
that short time to address the sinner and publican's prayer to
Heaven, and God knows I felt every word I uttered. It was one of
those dreaming sleeps where the mind, from the midst of danger,
turns to the happy past.

> 'I dreamt of my home, of my dear native bowers,
> And pleasures that waited on life's merry morn,
> While Memory stood sideways, half-cover'd with flowers,
> And restored every rose, but *secreted* each thorn.'

From these soothing and delightful visions I was roused by
the tenor voice of a young midshipman, who woke me from this
blissful state, by telling me that the captain wanted every person
on deck. 'What of the leak and the night?' asked I, putting on

my coat.

'Both bad enough,' replied he, in a tremulous voice. 'The one gaining slowly on the pumps, and the other losing its brightness, for no stars can be seen, nor the frigate's lights.'

'Why do we not fire a gun frequently?'

'The carpenter thinks it would have a fatal effect on the shattered frame of the barky.'

'May God keep off the wind!' said the youngster, 'for it requires very little to lay us in Davy Jones's locker,' and with this consolatory information I reached the quarter-deck, on which the sail-maker's crew were thrumming a lower studding-sail, by the 'light of lanterns dimly burning'; all the carpenters were repairing the launch by the same kind of light, and getting the boats ready, that could only bear one-third of the crew from destruction; a blue-light on each quarter was throwing its ghastly glare on the surrounding objects, while the noble ship seemed labouring with unusual weight, and much depressed by the head; her main-topsail lay to the mast, as the leak increased when pressed through the water. The clank of the chain-pumps, with the very faint cheers from those that worked them, was anything but exhilarating, and the great anxiety evinced for the sight of the answering blue-lights from Sir George Collier proved that our dangerous situation was not underrated. These sights, in the Bay of Biscay, on a misty November night, struck a damp chill to my heart, and effectually banished the beautiful visions engendered by my broken slumbers.

'Did you particularly want me, sir?' addressing my captain, who looked pale and agitated.

'Cheer the men at the pumps by splicing the main-brace; and harkee, water it, for fear of drunkenness. Send the first lieutenant and master to assist me in getting the thrummed sail under her bottom; under Heaven, that and Sir George Collier are our only dependence. What think you of the night?'

'A Scotch mist,' replied I; 'but no wind of consequence under twelve hours, and then I trust fair for Plymouth.'

'May God in his infinite mercy so order it!' said the captain, in a very pious tone, for in the course of my long experience, I have always found even the most reprobate turn to that Power that has controlled the winds and the waves, and put their trust alone in unbounded mercy.

At the chain-pumps, I found the men disheartened and fatigued, and the words 'beach her' (meaning thereby to run her ashore) escaped them, as the winches slowly revolved under their diminished power.

'It is an iron-bound coast,' said I, 'and in God's mercy, and our own exertions, we must trust. Spell, oh!' and a fresh gang took their turn at the winches. A blue-light and a gun from the frigate, gave us new life at the pumps, and a midshipman came down with the joyful intelligence that Sir George Collier was close up to us, and the fothered sail was under her in excellent style, and they were then hauling on the yard ropes to press it close to the leaks, which gradually sucked it in, and diminished the water one-half. 'Hurrah, hurrah!' and round flew the winches with life and spirit. 'Fill the main-topsail on her,' said the captain; and the noble ship again breasted the waters in gallant style.

A heavy weight seemed to be lifted from our breasts, and every eye beamed with greater animation; even the blue-lights which signalised Sir George Collier, did not cast such a sepulchral glare on surrounding objects, and the chain-pumps revolved and clanked with more spirit, as Chip the carpenter announced that we gained on the leak. 'Hurrah, hurrah, to get her dry out!' and the cranks went merrily round. It was most merciful that the wind continued very moderate, and even the usual Biscay swell had subsided in our favour. The slightest sea, in our shattered state, would have proved fatal, and anxious glances at the sky and barometer were very frequent. In fifty-two hours from the time of floating off the Pigeon Rock, off L'Orient, we anchored in Cawsand Bay, with the signal of distress, and in want of immediate assistance, flying at our masthead. This was answered by drafts of men from the ships of the squadron, who kept us afloat till taken into graving dock, where we entered with guns, powder, and stores. It was considered a miracle that a ship could float so rent and torn. Poor Sir George Collier, our stay in distress! I have dined in his company frequently, and a pleasanter companion could not be; and to think that a land historian of the sea, should make him a suicide! It is lamentable, and 'passing strange.' May the Power that strung his nervous system on so fine and fragile a make, look with a merciful eye on his rash and dreadful end! Pardon him, O God!

The Night Attack

The boatswain's shrill pipe, re-echoed by his mates, called attention, and 'Boarders away!' resounded through the decks of H.M.S. *Valiant*. It wanted an hour of midnight, and was intensely dark, when I ordered the boats to follow my motions without noise, and proceeded in search of a cutter, anchored between Rochelle and Rochefort, round which the boats of that division of the Channel fleet commanded by Sir Harry Burrard Neale were ordered to rendezvous, for the purpose of cutting out a convoy that had left Rochelle and been chased into a bay near that place some days previously. Its strongly guarded state forbade any prospect of success in daylight, as a very high promontory, called Point Du Ché, furnished with long thirty-two-pounders, afforded effectual resistance, even to the approach of an adverse squadron. A regiment of infantry were moved from Rochelle, and encamped round the very pretty bay, their white tents glittering on the plain, and giving more effect to its beautiful scenery. The admiral and officers that had volunteered on this desperate undertaking, had closely reconnoitred the place this day, and each officer had the plan of attack fully explained to him by Sir Harry, with the particular duty expected from him. The marine artillery were selected, and volunteers from that admirable corps, headed by Lieutenant Little, composed the forlorn hope. It was on reconnoitering we found that a regiment of infantry had arrived from Rochelle in the bay, and had taken an excellent position, both for defending the shipping and the promontory of Point du Ché. The plan of attack was skilfully arranged by Sir Harry. Darkness was the first requisite, and it was most essential that a landing should be effected, or the boats got so much under the promontory that the heavy metal with which it was bristled could not be depressed to bear on the approaching force. One hundred marines, commanded by their captain from the *Caledonian*, were to secure the retreat of the storming party headed by Lieutenant Little; and for that purpose were to take up a position between the boats and French regiment, whose encampment so much enlivened the plain. The boats were to move in six divisions from the cutter, their oars muffled, and each division having a different duty assigned them. Some were to board and cut out the shipping; others conveyed the storming and covering party; mine, in a seventy-four's launch, was to flank the marines, and, with an eighteen-pounder mounted in her bow, to check the advance of the French infantry. Now, fair and gentle reader, imagine the cutter – and she was found with great difficulty, not daring to show a light – imagine the cutter's deck thronged with the officers commanding the different boats, receiving the final orders of the youthful flag-lieutenant representative of the rear-admiral, each as he made his parting bow to the gallant youngster, for so he was compared to the senior officers under him, each drew tighter the belt of his sword, and placed his hand on the butt of his pistols. The quick ear might have detected the half-drawn sigh; and the rapid glance, had there been light, the slight suffusion of the eye, as some replaced the locket they had most affectionately pressed to their lips, arguing, from the dangerous nature of their service, a possibility of no other opportunity of bidding farewell to the much-prized tokens of love or friendship. At this moment some awkward fellow accidentally discharged his pistol, and the stifled exclamation of displeasure burst from numerous lips. All eyes turned eagerly to the dangerous battery of Point du Ché, and then swept the bay, where the regiment had encamped, but nothing denoted alarm. The sentinel still paced his lonely round, and a few minutes' observation convinced us they had not observed our unguarded conduct.

'Gentlemen, to your boats!' said our youthful commander, and they formed in the divisions previously planned. As we slowly approached the intended scene of disembarkation, for the strictest orders were given for silence, and the muffled oars just touched the unruffled water, we plainly perceived the sentinel as he stood on the topmost pinnacle of the high bluff cliff. His figure, as viewed by us so far beneath, appeared unnaturally large, and swelled out into gigantic proportions between earth and sky. Sometimes he would slowly pace the edge, then would he rest on his musket, casting a wary eye on the dark waters below. Every man held his breath, for this was the trying time. Death or victory hung on the vigilance of *that* man, and each eye strained to watch his motions. 'Hush!' was faintly heard along the divisions, and I thought I could distinguish even the beating of the heart, as the sentinel was observed to stop and apparently stretch himself forward from the cliff. A discharge of grape and canister at this moment from their heavy guns would have swept us like a flash of lightning from the face of the ocean. Thank God! he drew back, and, seemingly satisfied with his gaze, resumed his slow pace. Each person drew his breath more freely; at least I can answer for myself, who felt as if a ton weight had suddenly been lifted from my breast. Every yard had now life or death depending on it. Yet we could not exert more speed without drawing on us the attention of our wary and vigilant foe. With us all was profound stillness and inactivity, far different from the bustle and noise of action; and I am confident many a good resolution was formed, and many a silent aspiration ascended to the throne of Heaven for mercy. During the forty-two years I have been in the service, never did I feel my mind called upon for more fortitude than on this eventful ten minutes. Again the sentinel stood still, and stretched himself over the cliff, gazing on the deep, deep sea, like a man alarmed, for the dip of our oars had reached his quick ears. '*Qui vive?*' from his hoarse, manly voice, rang in our ears like thunder. Again we heard the challenge, quickly followed by the report of his musket. Now hissed the rockets as they ascended the sky, and the blue-lights in-numerable threw a ghastly glare on the frowning promontory and bay below. The grape and canister splashed and tore the waters into foam just outside of us, and the British cheer rung high and merrily, as our youthful commander shouted, 'Give way for your lives, men, and remember your orders!'

The divisions of boats flew through the placid waters, as the rowers bent both back and oar to their work; and as they neared the shore, diverged to their different duties. The forlorn hope, under the gallant Little, jumped from their boats, formed, and rushed up the steep to the attack of the battery with incredible speed. I drew off to the right of the marine corps, and directly in front of the French regiment, whose bugles at intervals could be heard above the roar of the heavy artillery and field-pieces, that thickly lined the beach, and now opened in earnest on the boats.

A sudden nervous start, and – 'I was afraid my right arm was off,' said the midshipman seated near me; 'but it is only confoundedly bruised by a shot striking the gunnel.'

'It is well you preserved it, for I want its assistance in training the carronade. So, oars, lay in the six foremost ones, bowse forward the gun, and load it with double canister. Now, coxswain, keep the bow of the boat directed towards the centre of that scattered fire you see advancing;' for the regiment had thrown out their sharpshooters to feel their way, and give some knowledge of the attacking force. Of these gentlemen I took no notice, confident that the main body were advancing in close column, and reserving my welcome for them alone.

By this time Lieutenant Little's storming party had gained the crown of the promontory, and were halted to reform, and gain breath, but finding the enemy endeavouring to turn one of their heavy guns upon them, the gallant Little gave the word to charge bayonet, and advance at double-quick time; sparks flew as they crossed bayonets, and many a gallant breast was transfixed by that truly British implement. At this moment their gallant leader received a ball in his sword arm, which shattered the bone, so as to require amputation, and the wounded hero was supported to the boats with the wreath of victory on his brow. The tramp of masses of infantry was plainly heard in the launch, and the sharp-shooters retired on their main body. 'Depress the gun, and stand clear of its recoil!' Nearer and still nearer came the heavy tread. I heard the command to our marines, to make ready and close their files. 'Fire!' and thirty-six pounds of small balls imperatively commanded a halt, which the Frenchmen acknowledged by prompt obedience. The flames from the grounded shipping that had been set on fire, now gave a glimpse of the retreating infantry, and our gun, by its playing, accelerated their march. The commanding officer now ordered the bugle to sound a retreat, and the marines rushed into the boats in double-quick movement. Never was a night attack better planned, or more ably executed. Our youthful commanding officer, now Captain Hamilton, then received his promotion, and we the thanks of Sir Harry Burrard Neale.

I feel myself called on in gratitude here to notice the extreme kindness of our reception by our excellent captain, now a full admiral, as he welcomed each officer by a warm shake of the hand, and 'Thank God, I see you all safe!' with the capital breakfast laid out in his cabin, to which I, for one, did ample justice. There is a warmth of feeling and susceptibility about a true Irish gentleman that is most pleasant to experience, and is excelled by no other nation on the surface of this fair globe.

The Mad Captain
(Rundel M'Donnel)

The inspiring tune of the 'Roast Beef of Old England' had just ceased its echoes through the decks of His Majesty's sloop *Racoon*, when her captain, better known by the name of Mad Mac, than the more Christian one given by his godfathers and godmothers, accosting me as officer of the watch, though I was first lieutenant – 'Keep her close in shore, *sir*.' And he stalked with all the stateliness of a new-made commander down the companion ladder. How the noble chief had attained the above cognomen I have no personal knowledge, but report whispered something of outrageous passion, nearly allied to insanity, and of the reef-point of a topsail shot from under the hand of the man who was tying it, by *his* pistol-ball. Be that as it may, from long experience I am convinced of the truth of the observation of a celebrated counsellor, whose out-of-the-way simile having excited the stare of the Court, pursued his address with – 'My lord, in fact all men are mad at times, and this has been my mad moment.'

Captain Mac's madness assumed the offensive form of pride and austerity, which nothing could soften but the magic name of a noble lady – some far-off cousin, a hundred degrees removed. This magical word sometimes procured me an invite, and a share of a bottle of claret from the great bashaw.

'Captain Mac,' addressing my superior respectfully, 'I think it my duty to mention that I feel it impossible, *being new to the climate*, to keep myself awake at watch and watch, and liable to all calls, as first lieutenant, both by day and night; and as Mr. Bennett has passed for lieutenant, we, that is, the second lieutenant and myself, hope that you will permit either him or the master to take the third watch.'

'Quarter-master,' said the captain, 'desire my clerk to bring me the Articles of War. Now, sir, you will be pleased to attend to this. "If any person in the fleet shall sleep on his watch, he shall be punished with death." So much for the first part of your request.

For the latter, the master and Mr. Bennett are not commissioned officers, and I am instructed by the Admiralty to intrust His Majesty's sloop with them alone.'

He issued a written order that no boat should leave the ship without his special commands, or sail be shortened without *his* directions. These orders we soon contrived to get rescinded in the following manner: – being all ready, we allowed the squall to press the ship on her beam-ends, and then loudly called down into the cabin that the masts would go or the brig upset, unless instantly relieved. This would bring a screaming command from the sleeping commander to let fly everything, and he for his own comfort, saw the necessity of leaving the shortening of sail to the discretion of the officer of the watch.

The sloop anchored off Aruba to water. This small island is the resort of smugglers, runaway slaves, and all kinds of runaways from the Spanish Main. The captain, after landing, let his gig return, *without note or message*. Towards sunset, the signalman reported the captain on the beach, waving his handkerchief. This conveyed an intimation, but could not set aside the written order respecting the boats, which we were told to obey on our peril.

'Are you sure, coxswain, that the captain sent no order about his gig?'

'None whatever, sir, but shove off and go on board.'

'Very well, Mr. Pipes; turn the hands up, and hoist in the boats.'

'Ar'n't I to go for the captain before dark, sir?' said the coxswain.

'Certainly not; for I have a written order that prevents me from sending a boat.'

The coxswain touched his hat, and, with a knowing smile, walked off.

When darkness ensued, a fire blazed on the beach, but the second lieutenant and myself were steady-going officers, and could not act on a surmise that the captain might want his boat, and send one in defiance of his written order. Oh no – we knew the service better. So, leaving orders with the officer of the watch to hoist out the boats at daylight, and send them for water, agreeably to his written orders before leaving, Dick Grant (the second luff) and myself joined our messmates at supper; and a merry supper it was, for one or the other of the mess popped their heads up the companion, to see how well the captain managed his fire, and their reports of its drooping, or burning brightly, were received with uncontrolled bursts of laughter, for his tyranny and oppression had turned all our better feelings into intense hatred. Let the censorious figure to themselves hell upon earth, and they will form but a faint idea of the misery of a sloop commanded by a *morose, tyrannical* disposition; then imagine the actors overgrown boys, and they will be near the truth.

At six a.m. the officers were drawn up on the quarter-deck to receive the captain, who did not appear with his usual neatness of attire, and looked pale with rage. The boatswain's shrill pipe manned the side, and the officers uncovered as Captain Mac stepped on the deck of His Majesty's sloop. 'I ask you, sir, as first lieutenant, in the presence of your brother officers, if you were not acquainted with my being on the beach, and waving for my boat yesterday, about sunset?'

'It was not only reported to me, but I saw you myself.'

'Then what could induce you to keep me all night among a set of villains that I am astonished did not cut my throat for my epaulet?'

'This order, Captain Mac, and the dread we all entertain of being brought to a court-martial for disobedience.'

He snatched the paper I held to him, and tore it to atoms.

'If I die of the fever I am now suffering under, you are my murderer; and, I fear, gentlemen, you are all aiding and assisting.'

And down he went to his cot.

The doctor in a short time relieved our anxiety, by information that his illness proceeded from suppressed passion, more than the fever of the climate. He recovered, but with no improvement in disposition.

This has been a long digression, but now to return to my tale. We were running off the wind along the island of Curaçoa, pretty close inshore. 'Captain Mac,' called I, down the companion, 'the course we are now steering will take the brig within point blank of Fyke Fort.'

'*Keep your course*, sir; and if the blackguards dare to fire on us, cast loose one of the carronades, and blow them into' – *I should blush to write where.*

'Gunners, clear away the foremost carronade; give it elevation, and point it for the fort now opening the point.'

At this moment a twelve-pounder from the battery whistled very melodiously over us.

'Their shot carry outside of us, sir.'

This communication was unnecessary, for the captain, with his mouth full, appeared on deck, and, with much spluttering, ordered the main-topsail to be thrown aback, and the people to quarters; and we turned to with a good will, and answered their fire in fine style, throwing a number of well-directed shot into the fort.

Our commander, who prided himself on his gunnery, now pointed one of the carronades, and fired, without taking out the monkey-tail. The recoil of the gun threw it with furious violence between his legs, and his escape was miraculous. 'A miss is as good as a mile,' said the captain; 'but what signal is flying on board the commodore?'

'Our signal to come within hail.'

'Fill the main-topsail – haul aboard the foretack.'

And we passed under the stern of *La Franchise*.

'I am delighted, sir,' said Captain Murray, 'with the way in which you scaled your guns; really it was very pretty firing; but I called you off, for fear an unlucky shot should cripple a lower mast or yard, as I cannot afford to lose a sloop so efficient from the squadron.'

Here the polished manners of the commodore got the better of his love of truth; for the discipline of the sloop was, as may be imagined, very so-so, and capable of improvement.

'Sir,' said my good-natured chief, 'this brig is in very bad order.'

'She is, sir,' replied I, pulling off my hat.

'Then the fault must be yours or mine.'

'Yours, sir, I think,' again bowing.

'How will you make that appear, sir?'

'In this way, sir; by every effort you have endeavoured to lower me in the estimation of the crew, and this conduct to the second officer is enough to disorganize a ship.'

'Give me an instance, sir.'

'Yesterday, Captain Mac, you ordered me, as first lieutenant of the sloop, to lower down the jolly-boat, and pick up an empty cask; when I desired a midshipman to perform that duty, you countermanded it, and obliged me to do it myself.'

'Oh! you are a bit of a lawyer, I see, sir, and I will avail myself of the first opportunity of breaking you.'

'Sir, I feel particularly obliged for your kind intentions, and shall guard against them to the best of my power;' and with a low bow I quitted my amiable commander.

The commodore made arrangements for storming the Fyke Fort on the night of the day that we had cannonaded it. A hundred volunteers were to land at ten o'clock at night under the command of Mr. Fleming, the first lieutenant of *La Franchise*. I was honoured with the command of our quota from the brig, namely, twenty picked seamen armed with cutlasses, pistols, and pikes. Our party drew up on the beach on a very dark night, neither moon nor stars visible. The storming party consisted of the same number of seamen from the four ships, and twenty marines from *La Franchise*, under one of their own lieutenants; the whole commanded by as gallant a man as ever drew a sword, Fleming, first lieutenant of the commodore's frigate. My orders were to keep the party compact by bringing up the rear. A Dutch guide moved with the forlorn hope in advance, composed of a sergeant and six marines, and were followed at twelve paces by the remainder of the jollies with bayonets fixed. 'To the right, face!' and we moved off the beach, striking into swampy ground at a brisk pace. In a short time we found ourselves bewildered among high canes. A halt was called, and the Dutch guide ordered to the commanding officer. I saw some confusion in the van of our small party, and heard along the line, 'Officers, to the front!' On reaching Fleming, I found the Dutch guide had escaped, by an imposition practised on the advance, that he wished to communicate with the commanding officer. From the height of the canes, and the darkness of the night, he easily contrived to elude the vigilance of those he had devoted to destruction. Great consternation prevailed among the staff, which was not lessened by the sound of an alarm gun from the fort.

'That sound directs us where we should go, and the quicker the better. Officers, to your posts, and keep your men together! Double-quick time, and follow me!'

Thus spoke our gallant commander; and the party pushed rapidly on, until stopped by a heavy volley, but ill directed, on our marine advance, who fell back on the main body. 'Close with the front!' was vociferated along our line. I thought I perceived a greater inclination for the opposite way; and by threats, with the point of the sword, had just closed with the front, when with a loud shout the Dutch party, who had fired on the advance, broke from their ambush, and crossed bayonets with our marine force. Lieutenant Fleming, who was at their head, received a bayonet through his jacket, which was flying open. The thrust, which was intended for his heart, was made with such force, that the Dutchman fell, from not meeting the expected resistance of his body; and as he lay prostrate and bare-headed, our gallant commander's sabre flashed, even in the darkness of night, and was in the act of descending on his head, when the Dutchman rose upon his knees, and with up-raised hands implored the mercy he ill deserved from his gallant opponent. The truly brave are always the most merciful; and Lieutenant Fleming stayed the uplifted weapon, and with self-possession that did him honour, collared the trembling wretch; and, under fear of instant death, compelled him to lead us to the Fyke Fort, into which we scrambled in the best way we could. As my muscular power was not sufficient to get over the wall, with my cutlass guarding my head, I, being then of slender make, contrived to crawl through one of the embrasures, and found the fort in possession of the gallant Fleming, who, if alive, I believe still remains a lieutenant up to this day; his noble captain dying shortly afterwards, his interest died with him![1]

When, with difficulty, I had crawled through the embrasure, all the time expecting my quietus in the shape of a ball, bayonet, or pike, as an intolerable noise prevailed, interspersed with sundry sharp cracks from pistol and gun, with pleasure I found myself again in an erect position, and taking a survey of the scene before me. In the centre of the fort, drawn up with military precision, stood the jollies, headed by their officer, conversing with Lieutenant Fleming, who was directing the seamen to prepare the guns – being seven twelve-pounders – to receive the flying camp of the Dutch commandant, whose fierce attack was momentarily expected.

'I am glad to see you, youngster,' said my bold commander; 'I feared you were among the missing or dead.'

[1] Lieut. J. Fleming was promoted to the rank of Commander, 2nd November 1814.

Some lanterns were making darkness visible, and in my hurry to reach him I fell over a Dutchman in the agonies of death: he had been shot in the groin, and in a short time expired.

'I congratulate you on your easy conquest,' said I.

'Easy enough, of all conscience. Most of the fools went out to lay in ambush; had they remained in the fort, we should have found tough work of it; but now we must prepare to receive the gallant Dutchman's flying camp. Take a lantern, and this Dutch prisoner will show you the magazine. See if they have cartridges filled; if not, prepare ten rounds for each gun; and be careful you do not blow us into the air, by firing the magazine. And, mister' – to the marine officer – 'throw out a line of pickets on the land side, the foremost one well advanced, with orders, if alarmed, to fire, and fall back on the fort.

Bearing a filthy lantern, whose dirty horn gave a dim light, I followed my guide down a flight of steps to the door of the magazine, which, having forced open, I found a great quantity of powder, and many rounds of cartridges already filled, and forthwith proceeded to make my report.

'Very well – we will hold this fort against any force they can send, till daylight, when, after blowing it up, we will effect our retreat, as we best can, to the boats; you, or the marine officer, visit the outposts every fifteen minutes, as the utmost vigilance is necessary. The sign and countersign are "Church" and "Chichester," which no foreigner can well pronounce.'

Agreeably to orders, I scrambled over the wall, and with a light and hasty step, a pistol in each hand and a wary eye, I approached the different sentinels, who, fully conscious of the necessity of vigilance, at some distance challenged with 'Who goes there?' – 'Rounds' – 'Advance rounds, and give the countersign;' at the same time making their muskets ring as they brought their bayonets to the charge position, and the clink of the cock fell sharp upon the ear. 'Chichester,' and 'All's well!' ended our interview, until I came upon the advanced one. He stood like a man thoroughly alarmed, and said he had heard female moans. 'Hist!' said the soldier, and the sobs and heart-searching groans, in the soft voice of the gentler sex, broke the silence of the stilly night. Led by these mournful sounds, I passed the sentinel, and in some brushwood I found a poor attenuated female, apparently of the half-caste, lying on the damp earth, with a dead infant in her arms. I conjectured that she had been shot through the body in making her escape from the fort, for her language, to me, was unintelligible, though her groans and shrieks spoke the universal one of suffering. I supported her head, and applied my canteen to her lips; the beverage, which she eagerly swallowed, seemed to revive her, and with the maternal affection so strongly implanted in woman's breast, whether black or white, she held her infant to me, seemingly unconscious of its death. I tried to raise her, with the idea of supporting her to the fort, but her excessive agony when moved obliged me to replace her, and I sat down, making my knees a pillow for her head. While cogitating on the best mode of affording relief to the poor forlorn one, for I dared not risk the safety of the whole party by taking the advanced sentinel to my assistance, I heard his sharp challenge uttered in tones of alarm, and his still sharper shot, with his hasty retreat on the fort. Being well aware that no quarter would be given by the Dutch commandant, with that instinct true to nature, though it went to my heart to leave the wretched woman, I again placed my canteen to her lips, and fled, and that with such good speed, that I arrived with the outposts, who came flocking into the fort, according to their orders. The man who caused the alarm, averred that he heard the measured tread of infantry, and the prancing of horses, but I think the beating of his own heart must have deceived him. We remained on the watch, and made every disposition for a desperate defence, and, as day dawned, laid a train to the magazine, and evacuated the fort, the marine force covering our retreat.

'A volunteer to fire the train!' cried the commanding officer, and several stepped forward. 'Here we must regulate by length of legs, and a capacity to use them. John Wilson,' calling to one of the volunteers, 'I have seen you active in running up the rigging – I select you to fire the train when you hear the report of my pistol; and remember you run for your life. Mr. Parsons,' addressing me, 'lead the party to the boats, which I now see approaching the beach. Quicken your pace, as I am going to fire the train in five minutes.'

I heard the signal, and in an instant there arose a volume of flame, overhung by a dense and heavy cloud, and for miles the island shook, as if from an earthquake, while the fort, with all it contained, was scattered over the face of the country. Our gallant lieutenant, with his long-legged coadjutor, joined us in perfect safety, and we entered our boats without crossing sabres with our flying enemies. Glad to find myself safe on board the brig, unpleasant as she was, I had scarcely refreshed myself with clean linen, when a letter was put into my hands, which caused great astonishment, and, in a great measure, displeasure. A youthful relative, in the first year of his apprenticeship, had quitted the plodding desk, and, without any permission but his own, entered in some West Indiaman from Liverpool, had got impressed by *La Franchise*, and was now serving in her as a mizzen-topman. He, thinking I still remained in the Channel fleet, where he had last heard from me, was amazed at recognising my voice while forming the storming party on the beach on the preceding night.

'And so, my dear George,' he wrote, 'I hope, from your situation and knowledge of the commodore, who is a perfect gentleman, you will induce him to take me on his quarter-deck.' This Captain Murray did, in the kindest and most gracious manner, censuring the youngster for not having made himself known to him before. I could have got him rated midshipman on board the sloop I was first lieutenant of, but I prized his happiness too sincerely to place it under the control of Captain Mac.

St. Pierre, the author of the most beautiful of all pretty stories, *Paul and Virginia*, very prettily remarks in his *Studies of Nature*, 'that where the great Creator places dangers, he likewise gives the means of avoiding them, by such signs as must strike the most careless observer; for instance, the sea breaking on rocks or shoals creates a white foam, and the darker the night, the more plainly is it seen; the voracious shark swims with a fin from his back considerably above the water, and is obliged to turn upon that back to seize his prey; and from the same beneficent principle and beautiful order observable throughout the creation, he makes the human countenance an index of the mind.'

The hard lines of cruelty and cunning were so legibly impressed on Captain Mac's countenance, as to become strongly repulsive, and I am convinced no human being ever felt, or could feel, affection for him; there was an affectation of suavity, and a smile playing round an ill-formed mouth, but it was hollow and deceptive, and truly verified the Scripture, 'that the heart of man is deceitful above all things.' His first appearance created in me a repelling sensation of disgust and dislike, which I found, on nearer acquaintance, daily augmented. How inexplicable is the attraction or repulsion of the human countenance, denoting in the gentle sex those amiable and endearing virtues which, old as I am, have inclined me to bow down and worship them as a superior race, nearer to angels than frail humanity; and to such expressive faces the heart fills with affection, and the hands spring to render service.

Blockade of the Island of Curaçoa

Early in the present century, the Hon. John Murray was entrusted, by the vice-admiral commanding in chief on the Jamaica station, with His Majesty's frigate *La Fortuné* and two eighteen-gun sloops, in addition to his own frigate *La Franchise*, for the purpose of capturing the island of Curaçoa, then a Dutch settlement, lying off the Spanish Main, and which the commodore pledged himself to subject to the British crown in a given space of time. It was my good or ill fortune (I have hardly made up my mind which) to be first lieutenant of one of these sloops. The proclamation of blockade was made in the *Jamaica Gazette*, and notice given to brother Jonathan, that any vessels found within a certain distance of the island would be subject to capture; but this did not check the philanthropy of our Yankee friends, who could not brook the idea of people being starved on compulsion, and very charitably used every means in their power to counteract our cruelty, by sending them provisions at five hundred per cent. increased cost. Commodore Murray, finding that the strictest blockade did not effect his purpose, and that the governor and his garrison, with true Dutch obstinacy, chose to live on, without showing the least symptom of surrendering to His Majesty's forces, now adopted the novel mode of landing a destroying party, from fifty to one hundred men, generally commanded by the first lieutenant of one of the squadron, with orders to burn everything intended for human food, shoot down all kinds of cattle, leaving the glorious sun to complete the work of spoliation – and to cross the island in the most rapid manner, by seizing all the horses in our line of march; and part of the squadron moved round to reimbark the destroying party after they had accomplished the good they had been sent to do. The Dutch boor of a governor, could not see the humanity of these proceedings, and wilfully shut his eyes to the advantages to be gained in becoming part of the great British empire. He, with unparalleled impudence, denominated our gentle proceedings the acts of buccaneers, and informed our commodore that he would hang up on Fort Amsterdam, as a pirate, every Englishman caught in these destroying parties.

The following night, the first lieutenant of *La Fortuné*, with his party of lambs, being busily employed in this work of destruction, were surprised by the Dutch commodore, at the head of his flying camp, about one hundred men, selected from the crews of their frigates in the mole, and kept encamped in the centre of the island under this active commander, for the express purpose now effected. Our party, only half their number, flew to their boats, leaving thirteen of their rear-guard, prisoners in the hands of their exasperated enemy. As no doubt existed of Mynheer the governor fulfilling his humane determination of making the innocent pay the penalty of the guilty, I was ordered away at midnight, with fifty men, under the guidance of a Dutch renegade, named Horsica, to seize all the principal men I could catch, to answer with their lives for those of our captured men. The first estate pointed out by that most exemplary traitor, Mynheer Horsica, was surrounded by our men, and a seizure of ten horses effected, upon which we mounted the officers and worthy guide, forming a small body of cavalry. The master of the mansion, with his wife, were declared to be in the town of Amsterdam. The house was of the superior order; and the mate of the *Fortuné*, who most probably was seeking plunder, with great glee informed me, that in a small room he had discovered three young ladies, daughters of the owner, endeavouring to secrete themselves. With the utmost speed, knowing the tender mercy of my lambs (something like Colonel Kirk's of old), I hastened to save them, and found the two younger sisters clinging to their elder one, apparently about seventeen – and all of them, in my eyes, beautiful – half-dressed, and frantic with terror. I saw some rudeness had been offered by the gazing, and armed, ruffians around them, and ordered them to draw up outside the house, in marching order, at the same time desiring Mr. Smart, the aforesaid mate, to put himself at their head. To this he demurred, and proposed the ruin of these unfortunate innocents. With some difficulty I disarmed the monster, and caused him to be bound to the back of one of my mounted sailors. The poor girls, who had fallen with fear at the angry altercation, and clashing of naked sabres, now crawled towards me, and on their knees watered my hands with their tears, bestowing many kisses on them. It is one of the few good and redeeming actions of my life, and to which I have often, in the hour of peril, turned with pleasure, that I used my best endeavours to soothe the terrors of these pretty innocents, and left them, as far as regarded us, in security and comparative happiness.

Horsica, whose angry passions were roused by the escape of the master, to whom I judged him no friend, advised, and in some measure commanded me to fire the house and outbuildings; but in the frame of mind I was then, I would sooner have burnt myself, and, with considerable pleasure, his ugly carcase; whose visage would not have disgraced the devil, displaying all the bad passions supposed to originate in that important personage. 'Close your files and move forward in quick time.' And with Horsica I rode to the head of our cavalry. He advised a rapid movement on the next house, a large farm establishment, from which we put in requisition twenty more horses, with the respectable farmer and his two manly sons.

Morning dawned, and displayed our grotesque cavalry, for all the sailors had mounted, and were not contemptible horsemen. We had eight Dutch prisoners, and Smart, the mutineer, to guard, with the dread of the Dutch commodore and his flying camp. Horsica said, a burgomaster, highly respected and of great note, lay on our route to the boats, and if we caught him, the lives of our captured seamen were safe. 'Here is his mansion,' pointing to a good-looking house not far distant, and we closed upon it at a hard gallop.

'Surround the house, and let no one pass,' called I to my mate, and with Horsica and two seamen, rode through a very pretty garden to the outer door. To repeated raps from our pikes, an upper window opened, and the head of a female, somewhat in a disordered state, was thrust out. To Horsica's peremptory demand for instant admission, a scream of fright from the demoiselle was our reply.

'Time presses,' said Horsica, 'force the door,' – and a post was instantly torn from its situation and propelled with great violence, as a batteringram, against it; three sturdy blows – bolts, bars, and hinges gave way, and Horsica, with myself and two orderlies, burst into a good-sized room, or hall, the bottom of which was composed of handsome Dutch tiles. As we had naked sabres in our hands, with pistols in our belts, it was very natural that the half-dressed domestics should fly in all directions; but Horsica intercepted an old woman in her flight, and, on pain of instant death, compelled her to point out her master's bed-chamber. Her exclamations, and entreaties not to enter, were in some measure ludicrous. Horsica explained to me that she said her master, Mynheer (*something*) had brought home a fair young bride from Amsterdam, only the previous evening, and urged upon us the impropriety of entering the bridal chamber.

'Call to him, Horsica,' said I, 'to come forth, and surrender himself.'

'And lose him for our pains,' said the ruffian, as he threw himself with violence against the door, that acknowledged his power by giving a free entrance.

A tall, genteel-looking youth, in the act of arming himself, met my view. He was agitated and pale, dropped the sword he was drawing, pointed one hand to the bed, in which lay his bride, and raised the other with an air of entreaty to Horsica. I caught a glimpse of a fair hand and arm, throwing the sheet over her face, as if unable to bear the view of armed men in her bridal chamber. To the young Dutchman's demand of what we wanted, Horsica replied, '*Yourself*, as hostage for the lives of thirteen English seamen, held by the governor under sentence of death, according to his proclamation.'

'I am a non-combatant,' said the youth, 'and not answerable for the governor's conduct.'

Horsica pointed to his military accoutrements. 'It is the militia, merely to enforce order, and protect us against slaves.' Horsica said, fiercely, 'This is trifling! Secure him with the other prisoners.'

And as our stout orderlies proceeded to bind his arms behind his back, his lovely young wife, conquering her sex's fears in the extremity of her distress, threw herself at Horsica's feet. He roughly repulsed her, and pointed to me as the nominal commander. I never yet could resist gentle woman's pleading eye, and least of all then, that I saw this lovely girl at my feet, her light auburn tresses partly shading the beauty of her strongly agitated and heaving bosom, her blue eyes fixed on mine with such an imploring look of anguish, and entreating for mercy. I did not understand the language she uttered, but the soft voice in which it was conveyed went directly to my heart, while the natural grace of her movements – *graceful because they were natural* – her unaffected terror, conquered by her affection for her youthful lord, spoke eloquently without words.

'Horsica,' said I, in strong agitation, 'I cannot consent to the slaughter of this interesting creature's youthful husband.'

'And yet you will to the murder of thirteen of your countrymen. I will not accompany any other party commanded by a boy – this business requires men. If this man is liberated, I shall instantly return to the commodore, and tell him that the tears of a woman are estimated more than the lives of your comrades.'

This, uttered in a harsh tone, checked my romantic feelings, particularly as I was fully alive to the importance of the prisoner. 'Then,' said I, 'speak in a consoling tone to this afflicted girl. Oh, that I could make her understand me! Say, her husband is in no danger, and will be tenderly treated,' and I took her fair hand to call her attention to Horsica. What he said I know not; but the tone it was uttered in grated on my hearing, and produced a wild, hysterical scream, with a frantic movement to clasp her husband. The orderlies, who had bound the youth's arms, would have repulsed her, had I not called out in a loud tone, *'Monsters, desist!'* – and I hastened to unbind his arms, with which he clasped his beautiful and youthful bride.

'Oh, *myn Godt!*' said Horsica, 'the boy is mad! Seize, and bind *that prisoner* to the *stoutest man that rides!*' and drawing near me, he hoarsely said, 'Will you load your soul with the murder of thirteen comrades, disobey your orders, and lose your commission for a woman?'

I felt the good sense of this remark, though it grated harshly on the excited state of my mind, and I closed my hand on my eyes to shut out this cruel scene. The devoted and affectionate girl was in an instant at my feet, embracing my knees, and watering my hands with her innocent tears, and I shamed my manhood by letting mine fall on her lovely head. The infernal, hideous voice of Horsica, 'All is ready!' roused me to my duty, and as I tore myself from her grasp, her maddening shrieks harrowed up every tender feeling in my heart, and, pulling my hat over my eyes, I sprang upon my horse and ordered a forward movement in double-quick time. We reached the boats, that fortunately had just touched the beach, in time to prevent the fierce attack of the Dutch commodore's flying camp, whose van-guard hove in sight as our rear-guard re-embarked. I threw myself into *La Fortuné's* barge with the prisoner, Smart, who came ashore in her as her officer, and now, with his arms bound, faced me from the bow of the boat. He maintained a dogged and sullen silence, which accorded well with my frame of mind. As Horsica had urged on me the necessity of shooting the horses that had rendered us such good service, and some angry altercation ensued, the whole of the prisoners under his charge went off to *La Franchise* in the commodore's barge, the young burgomaster looking peculiarly mournful at parting with me, his only friend. Arrived on board *La Fortuné*, Captain Vansittart inquired with great surprise the cause of his mate's degradation, and on my explaining his conduct, expressed the greatest horror and detestation.

'Wait till we have made sail' – for the signal was flying on board the commodore to hoist in the boats and make all sail – 'and I will teach him a lesson that he shall long remember. Mr. Evans,' addressing his clerk, 'disrate Mr. Smart to landsman,' and to the first lieutenant – 'When the signal is obeyed, turn the hands up for punishment, and I will give the monster five dozen.'

I afterwards heard he punctually performed his promise. I begged for the jolly-boat to drop me on board *La Franchise*, for I felt most anxious to interest the commodore for my young friend, the burgomaster. This request was complied with, and I stepped on board *La Franchise* as she bore up for Fort Amsterdam, directing the *Reindeer*, by signal, to cruise to windward of the island.

PREPARATIONS FOR AN EXECUTION

So many years have elapsed, that memory's log does not enable me to describe precisely, the person of the Honourable John Murray (whose sister, Lady Augusta, was married to his late Royal Highness the Duke of Sussex), but I remember well, that on entering the cabin of *La Franchise*, a tall, slender gentleman, much emaciated in person, and looking in extreme ill health, rose from the easy-chair, in which he had been reclining in his dressing-gown, and with courtly address answered my bow, saying, 'You are the officer, I presume, who commanded last night's party on shore?'

I again bowed affirmatively; he resumed his seat, and motioned me to take one near him.

'I am far from well,' said he, 'and very weak, which must be my apology for any seeming rudeness.'

This was unnecessary, for a more finished gentleman, with polished urbanity and suavity of manner, it had never been my good fortune to meet.

'From Horsica's report, I judge your feelings were *too* susceptible for the irksome duty imposed on you.'

'I hope, Captain Murray,' I rejoined, 'that I carried your intentions into execution in the most lenient manner that circumstances would permit. Horsica's advice appeared to me to spring from the disposition of a demon; and I feel assured, not only from your appearance, but from the high character for humanity you bear, that were you, sir, in my place, you would have acted in a similar manner.'

He replied, 'At your age I should. My remarks are far from intending to convey any censure; on the contrary, I highly approve of the feelings you evinced, and have liberated the youngest of your prisoners, on his promise to put the burgomaster's and other letters in possession of the governor in two hours. I have also addressed him, with official information, that those the fortune of war has placed in my power shall be hanged in sight of Fort Amsterdam, at the hour of noon, that is, should but one English prisoner suffer death in accordance with the proclamation the governor had communicated to me.'

'Oh, sir! would that you had been pleased to have made the youthful burgomaster the messenger, perhaps it might have saved from madness a lovely and most interesting female. Had you witnessed the agony of this picture of innocence and youthful beauty, as, with clasped hands and streaming eyes, she knelt at my feet, and with all the devoted and intense affection of woman's heart, implored for the safety of her youthful husband – Captain Murray,' I pursued, 'had the world's welfare depended on his death, you would have liberated him.'

The commodore here leaned his face on his hand, which prevented me from reading his mild and benignant countenance; but I saw, from the excited state of his nerves, displayed by his agitation, that he was strongly affected; and, being warmed, I went on to state the unutterable misery and agony of grief that she was now suffering, concluding with the following appeal –

'Captain Murray, I have faintly portrayed what I have seen; but for your future peace of mind, and for your soul's sake, take not that young man's life.'

The commodore raised his head with a slight look of surprise, sighed very heavily, and motioned me to ring the bell. He seemed near fainting, and his servant presented a restorative draught. He again bowed to me, which I construed into dismissal, rose, and with a low obeisance retired, heartily glad that I was not loaded with the same heavy responsibility that preyed so much on his susceptible mind.

I found the squadron under a crowd of sail, standing for Fort Amsterdam, distance three leagues, with the exception of the *Reindeer*, who had hauled her wind, and with tack and half-tack, took short boards to windward of the island, to watch our American brothers. Accosting a fine young man, who was officer of the watch, I asked if it was his opinion, from his knowledge of his captain, that he could have the heart to hang up eight innocent men.

'I have no doubt of their execution, should a single Englishman die by the governor's order, even if Murray's heart broke in witnessing it.'

'It will be an act of hellish cruelty,' replied I, 'and call down from just Heaven the vengeance of the Most High upon all the aiders and abettors in this most direful tragedy.'

'I do not see, sir,' said the young officer, 'how the commodore can abandon thirteen men to a shameful death for obeying his orders. He is a humane man, an excellent officer, and one of great determination; he has worn out a strong constitution in blockading this abominable island, and, in my opinion, is seriously ill.'

The lieutenant was right. Captain Murray died in ten days,[1] evincing, in the agonies of death, his love for his country, by ordering his body to be buried in a sandbank off Curaçoa, well knowing that his frigate could not be spared to convey it to Jamaica.

'Can I see the prisoners, Mr. Fleming?' approaching the first lieutenant.

'Undoubtedly, sir; show the officer to the Dutch prisoners.'

And I descended to the gunroom, where they were surrounded by sentinels, and attended by the chaplain, who addressed them in

[1] Captain Hon. J. Murray, son of the Earl of Dunmore, died 1st July 1805.

the French language, of which the burgomaster had sufficient knowledge to make himself understood. They all looked worn down by mental suffering; and as the burgomaster placed a lock of his hair in my hands, he earnestly made me promise to have it conveyed to his young and lovely bride, with information that his dying thoughts should be fixed on her alone, whom he hoped to meet in another and a better world. I wanted comfort myself, therefore had none to bestow on him, poor youth! but ascended the deck in time to see this smart frigate furl her sails, come to anchor, and square her yards, making signal for the squadron to do the same in close order. A shot from the mole, and one from the fort, proved us to be just out of reach of fire, but near enough to observe all passing on Fort Amsterdam, where the Dutch troops were drawn up in military parade, with the English prisoners in the centre of their square. The Dutch governor and his staff were on horseback in the fort, and masses of people congregated about it. All eyes turned on the British squadron, as they displayed the flag that had braved the battle and the breeze. The commodore hoisted a white one at the fore, and fired a gun; his gig then left the frigate with a truce-flag in her bow, and a lieutenant in full uniform, bearing letters to the Dutch governor from Captain Murray and his prisoners. As the Dutch boat received our truce-flag, our commodore, followed by the squadron, struck his flags and pendant half-mast, as mourning the necessity, and made the signal for the boats, manned and armed, to attend the punishment of death. At the same time eight yard-ropes were rove, and the carpenter's axe and hammer might be heard fitting the platforms over each cat-head. Shocked at these preparations, I obtained their jolly-boat, and returned on board my own ship, where all eyes were turned on the Dutch governor, upon whose fiat depended twenty-one lives. They had erected two triangles, on which lay a beam with thirteen halters displayed. The Dutchman and his staff, with spy-glasses, were keen observers of the squadron; and our commodore, with great tact, put his ships in mourning, tolled the bell as a passing knell, and ordered his bugles to play the 'Dead March in Saul'; and as they sounded mournfully over the calm bay, a shrill and piercing shriek was heard from the graceful person of the burgomaster's lovely wife, who with frantic energy embraced the governor's knees, and piteously begged for mercy on her husband.

He must have been harder than adamant to have withstood this heart-broken and drooping flower. I saw him raise her, and order the gallows to be taken down. The prisoners were marched to the mole, and embarked in a large Dutch boat; and as she pulled for the commodore, *La Franchise* resumed her flags at the mast-head, dismissed all appearance of mourning, and the crews of the squadron that were clustered like bees in the rigging, simultaneously cheered; and I felt as if a mountain had been removed from my breast.

Storming of the Dutch Camp

CURAÇOA

The signal to heave-to was flying in *La Franchise*, and our second luff brought on board the following order:–

> 'It being the intention of Captain Murray to attack and disperse the armed force under the Dutch commodore, now encamped in the interior of the Island of Curaçoa, you are hereby required and directed to select your quota of men and officers from those who may volunteer, according to the subjoined list; the whole to assemble on board *La Franchise*, armed with cutlasses, pistols, and pikes, an hour after sunset this evening.'

(Signed)   J. MURRAY

This order obtaining publicity, roused all the valorous ambition contained in His Majesty's sloop; and the whole of the company, from captain to cook's boy, volunteered on this important occasion. Our chief, who did not want personal courage, went to the commodore to tender his offer, as commander of the party, but with the utmost politeness he was informed that my gallant friend, Fleming, was already selected, in hopes he would render as good an account of them as he had done of the Fyke Fort. This wounded Captain Mac's pride, and he returned with his naturally sweet temper ruffled, finding me inspecting the party I meant to command.

'It is my intention, sir, to place my sloop's party under the command of the second lieutenant, and he will consequently select his own men.' Thus venting part of the spleen engendered by his mortification on me. At sunset the squadron made sail to close the shore, with the signal to follow the commodore's motions. Now, darkness covered the face of the deep, and we all hove-to, hoisted out the boats, and mustered in the attacking party, who were the *élite* of the ship, and had been busily employed grinding cutlasses, sharpening boarding-pikes, and selecting pistols with good locks, well flinted, each sailor wearing on his sword-arm a broad patch of white canvas sewed to his jacket, as a distinguishing mark. The whole landed at nine p.m., and were marched off the beach by companies, *La Franchise* and *La Fortuné's* marines forming the van, with an advance of four, under a stout sergeant of that corps; this man was immoderately fat for a sergeant of marines, and it convinces me, growing fat depends more on the temper, than feeding of the animal, whether it walks on two legs or four. Upon the fat sergeant's making out the encampment of the Dutch, he retreated on the main body, who were advancing with great caution.

'Did you see the advance sentinel?' said Lieutenant Fleming.

'I crept near enough to shoot him dead, but dared not risk the noise.'

'Can you seize and gag him without alarming the camp?'

'No; though the fellow seems to have neither ears nor eyes, the space is too open to cut him down, and he would not die without a squall.'

'Officers to the front!' and they collected round the commanding officer. 'Now, Mynheer Horsica, describe the position of the Dutch commodore, and what we have to encounter, that we may shape our measures accordingly.'

'All the officers,' said Horsica, 'with the company of the Kenny Hasler marines, sleep in, and garrison, a good-sized farm-house, built of stone, and tiled. It can only be fired from within; nothing combustible without, except the street door, which is African oak, and to which a flight of stone steps, eight in number, leads. On each side of the door stands a brass six-pounder, loaded with grape and canister, and the encampment of the remainder of the men is in rear of the house. I will creep forward and shoot the sentinel, and let the report of my musket be the signal for the assault.'

'Gentlemen, you have heard Mynheer Horsica's detail and plan of attack. I approve of every part *but shooting the sentinel*. The marines must carry the house and field-pieces; the sailors, equally divided, will move on the wing of the marines, and rush upon the camp. The whole will move forward in double-quick time at the sound of Horsica's musket. Till then, advance silently on the sentinel.' And the storming party walked with the greatest caution, till they could see the poor sentinel, who, unsuspicious of immediate danger, incautiously paced his lonely round. A slight disturbance in the nearest brushwood caused him to bring his musket down to the charge, and my informant (our second luff) was near enough to hear the click of cocking his piece. Horsica, whose ears were open, paused in his stealthy pace, and, tiger-like, crouched in his lair, while his alarmed opponent strained his sight to penetrate through the darkness of night. Finding all still, he hummed the fag-end of a song, and resumed his beat. The bloodthirsty Dutchman again crept on, and our party moved slowly towards him. The sharp report of Horsica's rifle, the piercing cry of agony, and convulsive spring of the sentinel, with the British hurrah, were all simultaneous with the desperate rush on the fortified house and camp. The surprise was most complete and successful, and resistance, except in individual instances, faint. The captain of marines of the Kenny Hasler rushed, half-clothed, to defend the street door, and was encountered by one of our marines, who brought his bayonet to the charge, and ran up the steps for the purpose of thrusting him out of the way, in doing which he stumbled, his hat flew off, leaving his bare head exposed to his adversary's sabre. The captain was a very powerful man, and with his huge sword, cut three times on the poor fellow's head as he was rising, and, strange to say, without penetrating the skull, which, I suppose, must have been comfortably thick, for the marine had sufficient strength left to pass his bayonet through his adversary's body, who fell dead at the threshold of his door. Fortunately for the Dutch commodore, business or pleasure had called him into the town of Amsterdam, on the previous evening, leaving the camp under the command of his captain, who was taken prisoner, with his two sons, and sent on board *La Franchise*. The field-pieces also were brought off, and the victorious party cut a great splash on the beach in the morning, with their prisoners and plunder. They were most deservedly cheered by the squadron, as they passed to their respective ships, and if their gallant commander, Fleming, still remains a lieutenant (which I fear is the case), I can only say it is a stigma on those who held the gate of promotion in the days of long, long ago.

The first person I met on my return to Port Royal was an invalid midshipman of His Majesty's brig *Go-along*, lately captured from the Spaniards, who gave me the following melancholy account of the loss of his captain and six prime seamen:–

'Our captain's signal,' said he. 'To dine with the commodore, flying on board the *Pelican*,' called the signal-man to the officer of the watch.

'Hoist the "affirmative,"' was the reply; and at four bells p.m., His Majesty's brig *Pelican* backed her main-topsail, His Majesty's brig *Go-along* having previously hove-to; and the captain, in full fig, came on the quarter-deck, and desired that the gig might be hoisted out and manned, to take him on board the *Pelican* to dinner. The officers assembled, the side piped, and the youthful commander, gracefully returning the general bow, stepped over the side, and into his gig, whose bow-oar was inimitably twirled by the bow-man, as the boatswain gave the shrill whistle on his silver call, and the sidesmen, agreeably to the signal, retired from their stations, unshipping the green baize on the captain's side-ropes.

'Oars!' said the commander; 'desire the first lieutenant to come to the gangway. Mr. ****,' addressing him, 'you will keep an eye on the commodore, and follow his motions.'

'Ay, ay, sir.'

'And I shall keep the boat.'

'Very well, sir;' and the first lieutenant replaced his hat as the young commander ordered his crew to give way. When the gig reached the *Pelican*, she filled, dropped her foresail, and stood off from the east end of Porto Rico; distance seven leagues.

His Majesty's sloop *Go-along*, literally complied with the orders left by her captain, and followed the motions of the commodore to the minutiæ of sending an additional topman aloft, provided the senior officer set the example. Shortly after sunset, the *Pelican* hauled her foresail up, and backed her main-topsail. The *Go-along* immediately hove-to, complying with the captain's order *too literally*, without closing the *Pelican*, who was observed to be rigging out her studding-sail booms, and shaking out a reef of the topsails. In a few minutes she bore up, under a cloud of sail, running free for the Spanish Main. Our observing friend of the *Go-along* instantly did the same; and, having the heels of the *Pelican*, overtook her about midnight; for it occurred to our sapient commanding officer of the *Go-along*, that it was unusual, to say the least of it, that his captain had not returned, particularly as the breeze had freshened considerably, and the *Pelican* was running too fast to tow a boat with safety.

'Ho! the *Pelican* ahoy!' hailed a loud voice from the *Go-along*.

'Hilloa!' responded the officer of the watch of that brig.

'Is Captain * * * * coming on board to-night?'

'Good God!' said a strongly agitated voice; 'is he not on board?'

This came from the captain of the *Pelican*, who, alarmed by the hailing, had sprung from his bed, and, in his shirt alone, now interrogated the querist.

'He left this brig in his boat, when we hove-to, a little after sunset. Oh, merciful God! he is, before this, food for sharks! Turn the hands up, shorten sail, and haul to the wind. *Go-along* ahoy! beat up to where we made sail from, and at daylight keep a good distance from us. I will give twenty pounds to the first man who discovers his gig.'

The commander then retired to dress, in great and visible agony and grief; nor did he, when dressed, leave the deck until the following evening, having during that time kept lookout men, not only from the mastheads, but from every other point that gave a view of the wide and open sea. During that eventful time, as the brigs crossed each other, many were the epithets applied to the first lieutenant of the *Go-along*, whom some did not scruple to consider as an intentional murderer, though I am of opinion this dreadful accident arose from sheer stupidity. Whatever the cause, the effect was dreadful, for, melancholy to relate, neither the young captain, boat, nor crew, were ever heard of more.

The *Go-along* bore the sad tidings to the commander-in-chief at Port Royal, and her first lieutenant delivered the captain of the *Pelican's* explanation.

The veteran Dacres, read the letter with great emotion, and our worthy preferred a request for the command of the brig. 'I cannot give you that,' said the admiral; 'but, if possible, I will give you something you deserve more.'

'Indeed, sir!' said the worthy lieutenant, with the blandest smile imaginable, 'what is that?'

'*A halter!*' responded the admiral, in his sternest tone. He then superseded the lieutenant, and sent him home to answer for his conduct.

———

Gentle reader! hast thou ever been attacked by rats, and felt thy blood run cold and thy flesh creep, as the repulsive

vermin have swarmed upon you? I have; and here commences
the tale of

THE RATS

Sir Graham Moore began the Spanish war, early in the present
century, by attacking four of their galleon frigates, one of which,
bearing a rear-admiral's flag, was sunk by his fire; the others he
brought into Portsmouth,[1] where the treasure was unshipped, and
sent to that emporium of the commercial world, London. The
prizes, being cleared of provisions and stores, were strictly
searched, and left bereft of everything, save an immoderate quantity of Bandicoot rats; but as an idea was entertained that the
precious metals might still remain in the linings of the ships, placed
there for the purpose of cheating the mother country of its duties,
by being smuggled on shore, I, with a sergeant's guard, was placed
in one of them, whose name I forget, for the purpose of protecting
such supposed property. I entered the captain's cabin as a winter's
sun was leaving the northern hemisphere, to gladden the hearts
that beat in a southern one, for it was in the month of December,
and not very remote from Christmas. The weather was seasonable,
for the snow fell fast and blinding; and the fire in the captain's
cabin, of which I took possession, was truly exhilarating; so much
so, that I strutted up and down it, fancying myself in command of
so fine a frigate, and even with the Spanish captain's trumpet,
loudly gave orders, with only myself to execute them. This did very
well till the lamp was illuminated. It was a large one, and threw a
flood of light over the spacious cabin. My cot I caused to be hung
rather high, or near the ceiling, for I had been cautioned that thousands of voracious rats, of the Bandicoot species, infested the empty
ship, with nothing in the shape of food but each other, and this
induced me to hang my cot higher than usual. I had, during my
castle building, when fancying myself captain of the goodly ship,
been startled by the strange and uncouth noises arising from their
preying on each other; but, being then too much excited and elated
by my waking dreams, I had no time to bestow a thought on my
agreeable shipmates. Having dispatched my cold dinner, and my
servant boy having retired to join the sergeant's party in the

[1] These three frigates were the *Medea, Fama,* and *Clara.* Their lading was valued
at about a million sterling.

gunroom, I drew my chair to the fire. With a book in my hand, a bottle of port wine by my side, I endeavoured to make myself comfortable; but

'Man *never is*, but always *to be* blest.'

And my comfort was greatly disturbed by troops of rats sweeping across the cabin floor, giving me a side glance, *en passant;* and laying down my book to throw something at them, I found innumerable small fierce eyes glaring ferociously at me, from all corners and holes in the cabin. This completely did away with the magic of Mrs. Radcliffe's vivid and romantic pen, and the *Mysteries of Udolpho*, on that night, remained still a mystery to me. I placed my drawn dirk on the table, my audacious neighbours seeming to take courage, as mine, like Bob Acres', began to ooze out at my fingers' ends, for I always entertained a great antipathy to the sagacious vermin; and pride alone, with a sense of its being unofficerlike, prevented me from joining the sergeant's party, from whom I often heard bursts of laughter, and the loud chorus of a song. I will take an extra glass of wine by way of a night-draught and night-cap, and by turning into my high-slung cot, raise myself above these infernal vermin, and laugh at their impotent attempts on my plump person. But first for a look at the sentinels, whom I found walking at a brisk pace, as the snow fell fast, and the cold was intense. Ordering that no boat should be allowed to come alongside during the hours of darkness, I returned to (I wish I could say) my cheerful fire, for shoals of those disgusting vermin were occupied in picking up the crumbs of diner, as I resumed my seat, and which I made a stepping-place into my cot, taking care to deposit my book and clothes in the same apparent place of safety. I lay watchful and restless, and heard the midnight guard relieve the posts, and by way of varying the scene, looked over the sides of my cot at my nimble friends, who thickly covered the floor, and on whom the lamp threw a strong light; but when I caught the ferocious and ravenous glare of their small eyes fixed upon me, my flesh crept, and my blood tingled at the idea of being eaten by them.

Putting up a prayer to that Power that alone can shield us from all dangers, with a heavy boot-jack in my right hand, I dropped into a sweet slumber; and it must have been profound, for when I awoke, from the pressure of the bedclothes, there must have been a considerable additional weight, as the white counterpane was totally obscured by dark-coloured rats, and one of the hideous brood was in the act of seizing my chin, as my eyes unclosed upon the frightful scene. With convulsive energy, I kicked down the clothes, and, throwing the boot-jack at the troops that thronged around and under my cot, ran, barefooted and undressed, to call the sentinels, and with their assistance transferred my cot into the gunroom among the marines, where the lonely feelings and sense of desolation vanished; but the horror with which the vermin impressed me is not yet effaced; and glad beyond measure was I to see an old buffer, from the *Royal William* guardship, come at ten in the morning to relieve me.

I told him my adventure of the previous night, but the old fellow smiled, and said I was young not to know how to foil rats. 'Observe how simply it is done,' said he, placing canvas over his cot, and sticking it taut to the sides, only leaving an aperture for him to enter, which he closed with a palm and needle when in it, in sail-maker fashion. 'Thus I defy your enemies, youngster,' said he; 'and their useless efforts and gambols will serve to enliven the scene, and take from the monotony of living alone.'

Gladly did I leave my sprightly friends in the hands of such a philosopher, and with double enjoyment did I relish the comforts of the well-ordered wardroom mess in His Majesty's ship * * * *, in which I then served as a third lieutenant.

Scenes in the West Indies

Four years after the present century had dawned on this small planet, bringing to it steam, gas, and all sorts of science, I was appointed by my commander, then chief on the Jamaica station, to a very old sloop there, to domesticate, among other pleasantries, with scorpions, centipedes, and cockroaches, a good-natured fag for second luff, a purser fond of bargains, and a captain very young, and full of fun and frolic. I had lately arrived on the station, and found Wellington boots, however valuable in England, not particularly conducive to comfort in that hot climate. After undergoing martyrdom for some hours with a very tight fit, quite new, the purser offered to relieve me from them at half-price. With soap, and boot-hooks, and many a hearty pull, he managed to encase his feet and legs in them, and then began his torture; for they, being long unused to a tight fit, thought proper to swell, and, from their enlarged state, refused to come out of their incarceration. All sorts of means were resorted to, in vain, and cutting them off was proposed, and rejected by the angry purser, who swore, as he paid for them, he would wear them; and accordingly turned into bed with them on, from whence his groans, exclamations, execrations, and repinings kept us in continual laughter; and at six a.m. the knife was applied, and he was relieved from great torture of body to endure the mental one arising from a commercial loss.

We were cruising off St. Domingo; the black brigands were pressing the town, and, being short of provisions, the governor ordered out the useless mouths, meaning children, and man's greatest comfort, the fair, the affectionate, the gentle sex, sweet soothers of our woes, and soft comforters in affliction, through good report and evil. These gentle and afflicted beings were, I am grieved to reflect, despoiled of their goods, and passed on to Porto Rico, or any other port they chose to wander to, without the care or trouble arising from property. Having amassed considerable prize-money from these exactions, we one night sent a mate and four men to take charge of a large sloop, being in chase of several others then in sight, with orders to keep as near to us as possible; but if he parted company, to repair to Oca Bay, in St. Domingo, and wait our arrival. On the fourth day, H.M. sloop cast anchor in the said bay, and a truly delightful one it was. Here thousands of cattle run wild, and with a large party I went into the forest for the purpose of shooting them. As the sea breeze fell, the scent of the wounded and dead oxen was offensive, and resembled butchers' shambles, more than the pure air in these delightful regions. The tall cabbage trees now began to obscure the twilight, and the English circular faces became elongated, while the smooth, open brow wrinkled, and lines of care and anxiety began deeply to indent themselves, as I ordered a return to the brig, and each man to see his arms in proper state for defence against any of the brigands, either black or white, that might be out in these extensive wilds on their predatory excursions; for stories were rife at Jamaica, of the most horrible atrocities committed by both parties, roasting alive at slow fires being cruelty of a low grade not worthy of particular mention in these days of horror; and a corresponding sharp lookout ahead, astern, and to starboard and port, while frequent councils of war, and cautions to look to our feet, as the sharp rattle of the deadly snake curdled our blood by giving plain intimation of its contiguity; while the slight raps from the elastic boughs regaining their position, as we pressed through the underwood, made us start and tremble, thinking the fangs of the reptile buried in our flesh. Cold perspiration bedewed my forehead as I called a halt.

'What say ye, men, are we in the right direction for the brig? and can any of you make out an opening to clear this infernal wood?'

'From the bearings I took of the sun when last visible,' said Mr. Pipes, the boatswain, 'we should alter course to port two points; but, shiver my timbers, what has caught hold of my starboard heel?'

At this moment a fierce rattle caused a revulsion of blood, with a faint cry of horror, and an apparent disposition to fly from the dangerous spot. Mr. Pipes made a forward spring, and the shrill whistle from his call echoed through the dreary wood, as he very distinctly piped belay.

'Boatswain,' said I, 'you will rouse the attention of some of the murdering parties, and our scalps may decorate their belts.'

'Better engage them, than a rattlesnake; but *hark!*' and the welcome sound of a gun boomed over the high cabbage trees, and the concussion shook the light foliage of the underwood. 'Thank God!' spontaneously burst from heart and lip, and we all pressed forward to where the sound appeared to come from. Our exertions were rewarded by the sight of the calm and lovely bay, with His Majesty's sloop riding majestically in it, her low black frame strongly contrasted by her tall taper masts, that gracefully reared themselves on high. Another shrill whistle from the boatswain's call, answered by his mates from the brig, ordering black and white cutters away, and most gladly did we step into the boats, but without two bullocks that we had attempted to bring in pieces to the beach. They had made their escape from the shoulders that had long borne them, to benefit the beasts and reptiles that infested the woods of Oca Bay in St. Domingo, named by the justly celebrated Columbus, Hispaniola. As the burning sun next morning rose from his watery bed, the signalman reported our prize in the offing, and as ten days had elapsed since we had last seen her, water and provisions were placed in the boats, and they were despatched to her assistance, as she lay like a log on the calm sea, her sails idly flapping to the masts. Approaching her, the boats, by the rapidity with which they made their way, drove off the sharks that had congregated round the hapless vessel. Countless fins might be seen above water (like a plantation of stunted firs) of these voracious monsters of the deep, attracted doubtless by the smell of the sick, and the bodies daily thrown from the vessel, for she was in wretched plight, without fresh water, and little provision. Never shall I forget the haggard and spectre-like countenance of the men, the helpless moans of the women and children, as they lay on the deck, exposed to the fierce rays of the melting sun, their tongues swollen and protruded from their parched and blackened lips, already the prey of myriads of insects – some eyes wildly glaring in strong delirium, while others were glazed and deeply set in the agonies of welcome death.

'Water! water!' hoarsely croaked the spectre of a man, looking wistfully at the breakers in our boats. Merciful Heaven! It was 'Thomas,' the mate, who only ten days back, with a 'John Bull' face, and a well-fed person, took charge of this prize, in which he had found a few gallons of brackish water, and above thirty women and children; the breaker that had hastily been placed in his boat contained six gallons of water, and that alone was pure and drinkable. It was soon, from want of due care and precaution, swallowed by the numerous parched throats that thirsted for it. Faint indeed, are the ideas of those who never experienced a want of this precious fluid, of the ecstatic delight given, in this sultry, indeed burning clime, from a hearty draught those will take who have long been debarred. It is a foretaste of the joys of heaven, and was forcibly expressed by the feeble eye lighting up with animation, and those set and glazed in death, again expressing gratitude and delight. One poor girl, apparently eighteen, had drunk copiously of sea water. If, reader, you have seen the animated skeleton lately shown in England, you may have a faint conception of what poor human beings may suffer, before welcome death brings relief. Alas! the inequality of misery in this best of all possible worlds! 'The proud man's contumely – the insolence of office,' *availing itself of its small degree of power to inflict all the injustice and misery that the little and low minds of vulgar men can visit on nobler natures.* But Dives and Lazarus will, no doubt, exemplify and equalise, or, nautically expressed, square the yards hereafter, and the longest life, compared to eternity, is but short, pass it how you will. 'Whatever is, is right,' says Mr. Pope; and I, from long experience, firmly agree with him, that 'there is a Power that shapes our ends, rough hew them how we may.' But a truce to digression. The prize was towed alongside, and the sick, by the surgeon and nurses, tended with careful kindness. The dead were committed to the jaws of the sea-monsters, that had hovered round the prize so long, and, as the mate stated, were not to be driven off with the blows their waning strength enabled them to strike; but each day, as they became more sickly and enervated, the sharks thronged and pressed upon the sides of the floating tomb, as if they were inclined to spring on its deck, and make the living, as well as the dead, their prey. How wonderful is the instinct of the brute creation, that can induce these large and voracious monsters of the deep, to keep up with, and constantly surround, these floating hospitals! I have heard of a shark of great magnitude, in Port Royal, that swam round the shipping in that port at noon each day, receiving from the men the offal of their dinner, invariably taken at that time. As this shark was a complete check on desertion, the officers would not allow it to be fired at, or in any way molested. In consequence, it regularly at noon might be seen, its fin above water, rapidly making its way to the shipping. He was named Port Royal Lion, and quite domesticated among the mariners that frequented that port.

Again we resumed our station off the town of St. Domingo, now most vigorously pressed by the black brigands, under their black chief, Christophe, who, upon one of our youthful captains being brought before him, on the capital crime of having effected the escape of a beautiful Frenchwoman, thus addressed him:– 'Sir captain, your life is forfeited by our laws, which must be respected equally with your own; I pardon you now, on condition that you report my message truly to your admiral, Sir John Duckworth, whom I respect, for beating our mutual enemy, the French. Tell him, if he chooses to put such boys as you in command of ships, not again to send them to trouble our free state; for, as yonder sun now shines, this is the last act of clemency they shall receive at my hands.'

So saying, his sable majesty rose with dignity and dissolved the court, much to the satisfaction of the culprit.

Shortly after four a.m., having the morning watch, my good genius induced me to heave-to, the weather being hazy and the shore indistinctly visible. As the day began to dawn, the cathead-man announced a squadron on the lee bow. With the glass I soon discovered them to be men-of-war, and laying-to on the starboard tack.

'Call the captain – turn the hands up – out with the reefs, and loose the top-gallant sails.'

By this time my commander reached the deck, and agreed with me in opinion, that they were a French squadron. This was speedily shown by their tri-coloured flags, in answer to our private signal. They consisted of seven sail of the line, under Rear-Admiral Missiessy, two frigates, and the same number of brigs, escaped from Brest. We were thrown into the utmost consternation, not being fit to fight, and unable to run, our sailing qualities being much impeded by the dirty state of the ship's bottom, contracted from her long stay on this station.

'Make all sail, and keep your wind close on the larboard tack,' cried the captain, who was keeping a wary eye on the frigates and

brigs that were shaking out reefs, and signalising their admiral for
leave to chase. Fortunately, he did not deem us worthy of notice,
and we passed, gunshot and a half off, to windward. When hull
down, we wore and made all sail for Jamaica, where we arrived in
due time, giving the admiral intelligence of a force double his own
on the station. The veteran anchored his flagship with springs, in
the narrowed part of the channel, and made the best disposition of
his small force to defeat any attack on Port Royal, at the same time
placing me in a fine eighteen-gun sloop, just arrived from England,
with orders to proceed to sea and reconnoitre the motions of the
French squadron.

The Sea Bear

On a bright winter's morning in the Christmas week of long, long ago, I joined His Majesty's ship **** at the mother-bank collecting the West India convoy. She was then considered a crack frigate, commanded by a sea bear, his dog, and his boatswain; and many of my compatriots will recognise the distich of –

> 'Duffy, the boatswain,
>   And Phillis, the dog,
> Rule the ****
>   Under a hog.'

In doing so – that is, joining this fine frigate – I came in contact with two excellent young men, under the same circumstances as myself – viz., ordered a passage out to the *Hercule*, the commander-in-chief's flagship at Jamaica. We were all young lieutenants, with Spanish prize-money in view, and a chance of rapid promotion, from pestilence and war. Short-sighted mortals! – the dictionary, now lying by the side of my desk, was the gift of one of them, his name Edward Maitland, and a finer young man never graced the naval uniform. Possessed of education superior to the common run of naval officers, who are taken from school and thrown on the world much too young (I entered the service at the age of eleven), the mind was equal to the goodly form, and Maitland was universally a favourite. On our arrival at Jamaica, the admiral appointed him to an active sloop of war, cruising on the north side of that island. She had anchored in one of the numerous inlets or bays. The night was calm and sultry when my friend Maitland had charge of the middle watch. Induced, from excessive lassitude produced by a first acquaintance with this hot climate, this officer reclined on a carronade slide, dreaming of his home, its dear native bowers, and still more precious inmates, when a scuffle, the clashing of swords, and death groans roused him. Disencumbering himself from his cloak, he called loudly to arms; but ere the words had quitted his lips, the sabre of a pirate was deeply buried in his breast, and the youth threw his dying eyes over a deck deluged with blood, caused by the lookout men, like himself, being asleep.

I can imagine, in some degree, the feelings of remorse that smote him in his dying agonies, from something similar that befell myself, who, at the age of seventeen, was made third lieutenant of a frigate on the Egyptian expedition, and in that capacity had likewise charge of the middle watch. The frigate was standing out from the sandy coast of the Great Desert, with a top-gallant breeze, the night serene and dark, the heat intense. After hitting my shins several times against the carronades, the slide of one looked so inviting, that I sat down, but it was only to be a minute. Take care, said Caution; life, honour, and property are in your charge. Only for a minute, and the words were on my lips as I dropped into a deep sleep, too deep even to dream of the happy home of my childhood. The shrill and sharp whistle of a shot, and the violent flapping of the mizzen-staysail, through which it had passed, made me sufficiently aware of the horrors of my situation, heightened by the cry of alarm from the lookout men (who had followed their officer's example) that a ship of war on our weather-quarter, was bearing up (for the purpose of raking us), and under our stern she passed, with her battle-lights fully displayed, while a stout voice bellowed through a trumpet.

'What ship is that?'

The captain, undressed, was on deck in time to answer, 'His Majesty's frigate *El Carmen*.'

'Who commands her?' responded the voice.

'Captain William Selby, who is answering you.'

'This is his Majesty's ship *Pique*,' said the commodore; 'and my private signals being unanswered for two hours, I took you for an enemy's frigate, escaped out of Alexandria. The last shot was directed at you, and I sincerely hope it has done no harm.'

'Nothing further than the loss of the mizzen-stay-sail,' replied Captain Selby.

'Very well; thank God,' said the commodore, 'that I did not fire my broadside into your stern, as I was on the eve of doing! Captain Selby, put the officer of your watch in close arrest, and report his name to me at daylight.'

'You have been asleep, sir,' said the captain, looking daggers at me, who stood silent and aghast, during this pithy dialogue, with feelings that could only be envied by the malefactor on the scaffold who has the rope round his neck. 'The penalty of sleeping on your watch, young sir, is death,' said the captain; 'go down to your cabin – and, sergeant, place a sentinel over the prisoner.'

Long were my cogitations whether I should save them the trouble of hanging me, by jumping out of the gunroom port, that looked invitingly open for my egress; but, on mature deliberation, I wisely determined to abide the pelting of the pitiless storm, throwing the onus on my superiors in wisdom as well as power. Although thirty-nine years have whitened my then auburn locks, I have a vivid recollection of my feelings, and can conceive those of my poor friend, Edward Maitland, as in his dying agonies he contemplated the consequences of his carelessness. The sloop of war had been boarded by a piratical felucca out of Hispaniola, which, from the want of lookout, had taken her for a merchant ship, and meant, by the massacre of her crew, to make her a prize, but finding their mistake, got away in the darkness of the night, leaving my poor friend, with many of the watch, dead on the deck.

Poor Edward Maitland, this little book was once thine, and the view of it brings to my mind's eye your goodly form, and open, animated countenance, when stating your wishes and your prospects, bounded only by the Union Jack at the main, for he had Scotch interest and great merit. Alas! his commission as a commander, and the news of his murder, reached Jamaica the same day. Peace to thy manes, my gallant young friend, till that dread time when even the sharks that entombed thee must disgorge their prey.

My other companion, to whom, as he is yet alive, like myself grey and probably bald, from the number that have stepped over his head, I shall give the name of Toms. He has lived, like me, to see the futility and folly of the sanguine anticipations of youth; and, like me, to endure the proud man's contumely with all that sears the heart and dries up its best emotions. But a truce to moralising, brought on by the recollection of my friend, and to proceed with my tale of the Sea Bear.

This man, in person and mind, bore greater affinity to the brute creation than the human species. His officers, unable to digest the coarseness of his manners and language, had all deserted him save one: and his first order to us, delivered by the sergeant of marines, is no bad specimen of his courtesy.

'Lieutenant Maitland, Toms, and Parsons, I am desired by the captain to tell you that if you do not instantly repair to your stations, he will send marines to force you up.'

'Unbearable,' escaped from the tongue of Maitland; 'we will seek the brute on his own quarter-deck.' And to it we repaired.

'Captain ****,' said my high-spirited friend, 'the matter and delivery of the command we have just received, must proceed from the insolence of your sergeant, as it appears to us self-evident that neither an officer nor a gentleman would send such a message, by such an unusual messenger, to officers on half-pay, ordered a passage, and who had not the slightest intimation of your wish for their active services.'

To this the Bear growled in gruff tones, 'Mister, have you stationed these young men?'

'No,' said Mister, who had very lately joined in the capacity of first lieutenant, and a more gentlemanly officer never graced the situation – 'No, sir; I could not think of doing so without your orders.'

'Then damn you, sir, I will show you your duty by performing it myself. Here, you, Mister,' growled Bruin, not in the most dulcet tone, addressing his growl to me, 'you, I suppose, would like to eat the bread of idleness; your station is the forecastle, and yours the waist,' looking at Maitland; 'and yours, Mr. Toms, the quarter-deck – you shall have charge of the watches; and, by –,' irreverently using the name of the Most High, 'if you do not do your duty, I will break your bread. Now, that is my answer to your insolent speech, young sir. My eye is on you.'

We were then unmooring, as the signal for sailing was flying on the flagstaff at Portsmouth. At this moment, a fine, manly boy, now high in rank, and an ornament to the service, made his bow to the Bear, and announced his return on board.

'Where is the doctor?' growled Bruin.

'I found him confined to bed, sir, apparently very ill; and his medical attendant assured me that removal, in his present state, would affect his life.'

'My order to you was to bring him on board, dead or alive, and I sent two files of marines to enforce it. Sir, you have disobeyed that order, and your duty henceforth is in the foretop. Mr. Quillum, degrade that midshipman to the rank of landsman; and, Mr. Duffy, keep a sharp eye on him.' He then looked to the boatswain, who flourished his stick in token of approbation.

The youth, who, till now, had stood respectfully uncovered, replaced his hat, while his eyes flashed angry defiance at the Bear.

So to sea we went, for the pestilential climate of Barbados and Jamaica, without a medical man of any description on board, though our passengers consisted of a general officer and his staff, the major of whom whispered to me during the above scene, 'I thank my God I am not in the navy.' We had also a commissioner of seventy-five, with a wife of twenty-five, to whom the major paid great attention.

Running through the Needles, with a convoy of more than a hundred sail, which we speedily diminished to half a dozen, and finally arrived solus, we had not been long on the passage, when the crowded state of the maindeck, from the unusual quantity of two-year-old heifers that Bruin was taking out on speculation, cramped the men in their pastimes; and three of the finest beasts were found dead one morning, having been choked by Guernsey frocks, well greased, during the night. The roaring of the Bear was alarming to the lady commissioner, who declared that it would deprive her of appetite to look at meat not killed in the regular way; for Bruin had ordered it to be cured and cooked for his own table. He was a miser, and a sordid one.

'Captain,' said the general, 'you have a handsome sum allowed for my passage, and it is painful to me to be obliged to hint that we guardsmen are used to gentleman's fare.'

'The beef is good,' growled Bruin; 'I eat of nothing else – other food shall be provided for you.'

'Then I trust it will appear on your table in an undisguised state.'

'It shall,' growled Bruin.

The officer of the forenoon watch invariably dines with the captain; and the day the above treaty was concluded I had that watch, being the only one of the three that could put up with the gross language of the Bear.

'Damn you, sir,' said he to Toms, 'you are taking in that sail like a lubber.'

'I am entitled to respect as officer of the watch,' said Toms; 'and I will not continue to do duty under such language.'

'Oh, mutinous!' growled the Bear. 'Consider yourself a prisoner; and allow no intercourse with him,' to the officer of the guard. 'He must swing for this at the foreyard.'

My friend Maitland wisely got sick, and the sudden change of climate had affected my health.

'How do you feel yourself to-day?' growled the Bear, throwing open the cabin door. 'Let me see, are you fit for duty?' And he went through the farce of feeling our pulses. 'You are better; I knew the draught and pills I sent you would effect a cure.' Then it must have been on the fish, thought I, if any could be so foolish as to swallow them; as upon their receipt I consigned them to the deep, deep sea. 'I will put you out of the sick-list tomorrow; those pills answer with every person but you,' looking hard at Maitland, who, like myself, wished the fish to receive every benefit they could render. 'I will try another system with your stubborn constitution.'

And the Bear rolled off, accompanied by his dog Phillis, who, in appearance, was worthy of her master, the ugliest cur, snappish and crossgrained; yet the beast had a hammock slung in the captain's cabin, and was most carefully put to bed at early hours.

As the sight alone, of those miraculous pills had cured me, I was struck out of the sick-list, and kept the forenoon watch on the day of the hollow truce established between the captain and general.

'I will lay you a small bet, major,' said I, as we paced the quarter-deck, 'that the captain will not fulfil his part of the agreement; and I will ascertain, when relieved at noon, the different compositions of his hospitable board.'

Accordingly I examined Quashie, the black cook, whose reply was, 'A very good dinner, sare, very good; there is a sea-pie.'

'What is it made of, Quashie?'

'Fowls, mutton.'

'What, no beef, Quashie?'

'Yes, massa, plenty of beef, massa; but I no peak.' And Quashie laughed in his peculiar manner.

I saw directly, that the spirit of the treaty was violated, and gave information to the major, who was very indignant.

This occasioned an angry remonstrance, and the early breaking up of our dinner-party. The captain, by a conference with his steward, having understood my share in the disclosure of his ingenious mode of feeding his guests, ordered a reef to be taken in the topsails. 'I will show you how to perform that duty, Mister, as I wish it done,' said he to the first luff. 'Mr. Duffy, all hands reef topsails.' He, after a shrill whistle, repeated, 'All hands reef topsails, ahoy; tumble up there, fore and aft.' And the top-men placed themselves in the rigging. 'Away aloft.' And up they flew. 'Let go the bow-lines and lower away the topsails. Why don't you let go the fore-topsail haulyards forward?'

'They are gone, sir,' said I.

'They are not gone,' roared he; 'or else your lifts are foul in the chains.'

'All clear, sir; all gone,' replied I, respectfully; 'the weather-brace wants rounding in to spill the sail.'

'I say you lie, sir,' roared the Bear, and he approached me, foaming at the mouth with passion, and flourished his trumpet as if with an intention of striking me down.

With folded arms, to indicate that I made no resistance, I pointed out everything clear; but, stamping on the deck, he ordered a cabin to be fitted for me on the main-deck, there to remain a close prisoner under the charge of a sentinel.

Upon this order I made no comment, but walked directly to the gunroom, where the marine officer, now high in rank and an ornament to his profession, soon came to express his regret that he was compelled to enforce the captain's orders, which were to place me in close confinement between two guns, on the main-deck. To this arbitrary and unusual proceeding I expressed my dissent in strong terms, declaring that nothing but physical force (to which I would oppose all the resistance in my power) should induce me to quit the gunroom, to which my situation as lieutenant of the *Hercule* entitled me, under an Admiralty order, for a passage. The high rank of his passengers, and their unfavourable disposition towards him, who had styled the general a glutton and the commissioner an old fool, was a check on the brute's further proceedings, and I carried my point of associating with my messmates.

The frigate had many supernumerary midshipmen, and the fate of one of them was so peculiarly tragic, that I trust my readers' patience will follow me through the detail of what happened 'long, long ago.' This young gentleman had come out on the prospect of being provided for by the yellow fever (a strong auxiliary of the Admiralty in silencing importunate claimants) or promotion. He got the latter by hard service and good conduct, and was appointed to command the *Magpie* schooner, that carried more sail than ballast. One morning, at the east end of Jamaica, she was surprised by that curious phenomenon, a waterspout, that threw her completely over, and the schooner disappeared, leaving the commander, twelve men, and her boat, that fortunately had not been lashed, floating on a calm, unruffled sea. The commotion occasioned by the whirlwind having subsided – 'Right the boat, men, quickly, for your lives; the sharks – the horrid sharks – will be upon us.'

The boat was floating bottom upwards, and eager hands and shoulders succeeded in righting her, but in such a hurried way as to be nearly full of water, and in consequence very tender (that is, easily upset). The lightest and most active lad was now ordered by the commander to get into the boat, and commence baling with his cap, the only thing available among these unfortunates, he having raised him with one hand for the purpose; the youth, with convulsive shuddering, uttered the dreadful word 'Shark, shark!' fell down on the gunwale, and again the boat turned bottom upwards. The splash, and desperate efforts of the crew, for they worked as despairing men of strong sinews will work, to escape the dreadful fate so closely impending, in some measure scared and altered the direct attack of the monster, who swerved, and swept in circles round the hapless beings, showing his hateful fin high above the troubled waters, before so placid. 'Shout loudly, men,' cried the officer, 'and bale away, lad, without looking at the shark' (who kept narrowing his circles, as he swiftly passed around them). 'God is able to deliver us, even in this great extremity; avoid getting into the boat until she is more buoyant, but splash the water about with all the noise you can make.'

A violent rush, a terrific scream of agony, and the disappearance of one of the stout seamen, followed by a crimson tinge on the waters, attested the voracity of this scourge of the sea. 'He will gorge himself on poor Tom,' said the commander, inexpressibly shocked, 'and we are freed, if the blood' (here he checked his disclosure, for he well knew that the scent of blood would draw myriads around them). 'Lift Jack carefully in too; bale with your hands,

Jack – quickly, quickly; for I see their dreadful fins appearing all around. Oh! God of mercy, shield us!'

Another rush, and piercing shrieks curdled their blood, as the fish, with difficulty, drew an herculean, well-formed man beneath the surface. All was now wild commotion; caution and order had given place to paralysing fear, and each man grasped madly at the boat; but, providentially for those in her, the ravenous monsters carried off in their jaws every floating man before he could upset the boat in his mad efforts to save himself from the horrible death in view. The violent struggle of the monsters for their prey, when two of them seized the same person; the imprecations and ofttimes prayers of those in the boat, which floated in a sea of blood, as they attempted, by stretching their hands, to save their sinking shipmates, who, with starting eyeballs and wild gestures, cried to them for succour; the scene is too terrific further to contemplate, or fully attempt to portray; the dread reality is often endured by those 'who go down to the sea in ships, and occupy their business in the great waters.'

The wretched youth in command, was, by the exertions of the lads in the boat, extricated from the jaws of two ravenous monsters, each of whom had seized and carried off a leg, and the bleeding trunk of the youth was hauled into the boat, to undergo a more languishing death from loss of blood. The poor boys, nearly dead with fear and apprehension, did their best to stop the bleeding, by passing some rope yarns round the stumps, which were greatly shattered and jagged by the teeth of the monsters, who had apparently splintered the thigh bone up to the hips. Heavy groans attested the sufferings of the hapless youth, but they got fainter and fainter as the extended his hand towards the island, with an imploring look of anguish, till welcome death relieved him from his intolerable misery.

The death of their commander, under such shocking circumstances, left the youths (for they were but striplings), in comparative quietude. With heads bowed upon their knees, and hearts paralysed with fear, and nearly broken from the distressing scenes they had witnessed, afraid to look each other in the face, where ghastly despair sat enthroned, they shuddered at every shock the boat sustained from the ravenous fish jostling and crossing her in all directions, being attracted by the scent of blood issuing from the ill-fated commander. 'The devils will be in the boat, or upset her, if we do not throw the body to them; lend me a hand, Tom,' and overboard went the useless trunk of a formerly good-looking youth, but a few hours since loving and beloved. Most true that 'in the midst of life we are in death.' The disappearance of a host of fins, diving for the body, gave breathing time to the lads, who threw a despairing gaze on the wide and open sea; the loom of the blue mountains, seen in the distance, alone soothed their inquietude; but they were devoid of any means of reaching it; no oars, no sails, and, the worst of all the negatives, no fresh water. But they dipped their upper garments alongside, and placed them on their fevered bodies, by which they absorbed moisture sufficient to keep them from maddening with thirst. One of our numerous cruisers fortunately took them on board – more fortunate than the *Go-along's* gig, who, with the captain and crew, have never yet been heard of, though it happened long, long ago.

This is a long digression from the subject of my friend Bruin, whose acts are chronicled in the West India memories of that period. We reached Barbados at so sickly a time, that not a medical man could be procured, though a frigate lay in the bay; but she had buried the captain, and two lieutenants out of the three; while we, without any person save the captain (whose physic nobody but the fish took), in the shape of a doctor, were perfectly healthy, and lost not a man until we reached Port Royal, when we recruited our medical staff, and the yellow fever followed, making great ravages among the youthful part of our community. One of its victims I much lamented, the handmaiden of the old commissioner's young wife. To think that the land crabs should feast on that beautiful form, and deface that cheek that rivalled the peach in bloom! in fact, she was one of those roses so common to English peasantry. Animated with delight at the prospect of seeing the world, she left her cottage and happy home, to feed the most frightful vermin that infest the palisades of Port Royal, useful in acting as scavengers to the burying-ground, so dominated. In the words of Mrs. Hemans, I address her sorrowing mother:–

'But there is a world that knows no blight,
You will find her there with her eyes of light,

When ye go where the loved who have left ye dwell:
This flower is not death's; fare ye well, fare ye well.'

When the high lands of that beautiful island, Jamaica, called the Blue Mountains, showed their heads above the deep blue sea, Bruin assembled all the mutinous, seditious, and contumacious officers he had carried out under arrest, with the now post-captain (then acting as foretopman of the frigate), and addressed them as follows:– 'Gentlemen, some of you I could hang, and the others I could break their bread; but you are all young, and my disposition is merciful (no person was before aware of it!). I shall say nothing further of your faulty conduct – you are at liberty. And, Mr. Quillum, restore Mr.**** to his grade as midshipman. You will resume your station on the quarter-deck, sir, and strictly obey your orders in future.'

Thus amicably concluded my service with the Bear, his dog, and his boatswain. The only officer who stuck by the frigate was a young lieutenant, who had great interest, as a relative of Mr. Pitt's, then Prime Minister, and, consequently, every reason to expect rapid promotion in that unhealthy clime. He was sociable, good-natured, and talented, giving indications of a master mind; but the resistless fever bowed his lofty head, and he was carried to the palisades, making use of the language recognised there, 'as a gemman, and not like kaley beggar.' It costs about one hundred pounds to merit that eulogium.

On appearing before the commander-in-chief, who had worked his way upward by dint of hard service and good conduct, to his present high station, he seemed at a loss what to do with so many supernumerary officers as His Majesty's frigate poured upon him, and all appointed to his flagship. 'You must remain on board the frigate for the present,' said the admiral, 'till I can see in what manner I can best place you for the advantage of the service. In you I recognise one of my youngsters in the *Barfleur* and *Foudroyant*.'

The veteran[1] had been my captain in those ships from the early part of the year 1795, and a kind-hearted, worthy man I found him; he had struggled through a long life of difficulty, made an excellent fortune during the Spanish war, got thrown from his horse,

[1] Vice-Admiral J. R. Dacres.

lingered, and died; but previous to this finale he appointed me first lieutenant of the old sloop, commanded by the young captain, now a flag officer of very high repute, and most deservedly a Knight Commander of the Bath. Having battered both hat and head, until I had learnt to practise a stooping position, so necessary to the accommodation afforded by this old sloop, and endeavoured to be on peaceable terms with the scorpions, centipedes, and cockroaches, that infested her, I substituted a jean jacket for my coat, and took my station, as appointed, in the gunroom at dinner, with a most facetious, pleasant fellow for a doctor, in addition to the messmates formerly commemorated in scenes in the West Indies. 'As you are a Johnny Newcome,' said the doctor, after the toast of 'a bloody war and a sickly season' had been duly honoured, with some interesting information relative to the dead, the dying, and the convalescent, 'I conjecture you have not heard the story of the pig.'

'I have not yet had that pleasure,' replied I.

'Good,' said he, rapping the table as a call of attention. 'Silence, gentlemen, while I enlighten the obtuse intellects of this greenhorn. Once upon a time, and that at not a very remote period, our dear country, young gentleman, possessed an admiral, famous in story, and standing high as a valiant and fortunate officer, much renowned in arms; but as nothing human is perfect, this admiral possessed an alloy, like a spot in the sun, that sullied his brightness; he was very covetous (an anti-seamanlike vice), and, for the sake of filthy lucre, carried a number more pigs than were required for his own table, to fatten on His Majesty's pea-soup, served out at the hour of noon in His Majesty's ships. The ship bearing his flag was cruising not a thousand miles distant of the latitude and longitude we are now in, and with top-gallant sails, courses, and jib, was, on a beautiful day, standing inshore with the squadron he commanded. All at once this far-famed officer appeared on the quarter-deck, agitated, and without his hat.

'"Shorten sail and heave-to, sir," commanded he, in peremptory tones; "lower down a boat, and save the pig. I am astonished at your want of look-out, and your want of humanity, in leaving the poor pig to be gobbled up by the sharks. Be handy with the boat, sir."

'"Ay, ay, sir!" said the officer.

'"Watch and idlers, shorten sail, pipe the yellow cutter away there."

'In the midst of the bustle thus created, the admiral's steward whispered his master, "The pig, sir, is not yours, but belongs to the wardroom."

'"Are you quite sure?"

'"I am, and have just counted yours."

'"Fill the maintopsail again, and make sail – keep fast the boat. Poor piggy, you must die," throwing on the pig a glance of great commiseration.

'The admiral had a character for humanity and kindness of heart, and appeared much shocked as he saw a shark about four yards long make a narrow circle round the animal, who showed wonderful instinct and terror of his dread foe, and made a clean leap out of the water. As the monster darted upon him, the snap of his teeth was heard as he closed his ponderous jaws on the hind quarters of poor piggy, leaving the water much discoloured, and the death shriek, or squeak of agony, ringing in the admiral's ears.'

'Capitally told, doctor. Gentlemen, I propose the doctor's health in a bumper, with three times three,' said my commercial mess-mate, the purser, who had not then purchased the tight fit I hereafter obliged him with.

'Johnny Newcome, my boy,' called the doctor the following morning, 'mark that officer pulling seaward?'

'I do. A stout, gentlemanly, good-looking, young and healthy man.'

'The land-crabs will eat him in less than a month; mark my words. He is a man of great interest, sent out to be the first promoted, and fortified against the climate by the sage advice of the cleverest doctors in London; and in compliance with that, he is drinking his spruce, and inhaling the sea breeze. To prevent the yellow fever, is constantly on his mind, and gives a predisposition to take it. He will only require six feet on the palisades in half that number of weeks.'

The doctor was perfectly right, and his prediction was fulfilled with unerring accuracy.

Tom Allen

Death has lately swept from Greenwich Hospital the above-named Tom Allen, celebrated by Captain Chamier, under the title of 'Ben Brace,' the last of the Agamemnons. He was the faithful body-servant of the great Lord Nelson, when I was his signal-midshipman in the *Foudroyant*. Selected from the waist of the *Agamemnon* by Lord Nelson for some daring deed, and constituted his valet or gentleman out of livery; clumsy, ill-formed, illiterate, and vulgar, his very appearance created laughter at the situation he held; but his affectionate, bold heart, made up for all deficiencies; and, next to Lady Hamilton, Tom Allen possessed the greatest influence with his heroic master.

'You' (or, as he in his Norfolk dialect pronounced it, *yow*) 'are to dine with my lord to-day,' said he to me on the anniversary of the fourteenth of February.

'I cannot, Tom, for I have no clean shirt; and we have been so long cruising off Malta, that my messmates are in the same plight.'

'But yow must, for my lord insists on meeting all those that were at the battle of St. Vincent, at dinner, this day.'

'Make the best excuse you can for me, Tom, for I really cannot go.'

Away waddled Tom, very much like a heavy-laden ship rolling before the wind, and the best excuse the simplicity of his mind suggested was the truth.

'Muster Parsons has no clean shirt, and he coon't dine with you to-day.'

'What ship was he in, Tom?'

'The *Barfleur*.'

'Then tell him to appear in my cabin in the one he has now on, and he may send the first clean one that comes into his possession for me to look at.'

Thus saying, the admiral resumed his pace, conversing with Captain Hardy on the possibility of attacking the French fleet of twice our force, then lying in Vardo Bay.

'If the Portuguese were but English' – (Lord Nelson here alluded to the Marquis de Neiza's squadron, six sail of the line, acting with our fleet) – 'if they were but English, Hardy, we would beat them like stock-fish. As it is, I long to be at them, for I do not feel easy in cruising off Marittimo with twelve fine ships of the line (not counting our friend the marquis's squadron, who is good for something), while thirty of them brave us in Vardo Bay. What say you, Hardy? shall we have at them, sink or swim? We ensure a monument in Westminster Abbey.' And frequently the gallant admiral has been heard to exclaim, while pacing the deck occupied by his own reflections, and in imagination fighting the battle in Vardo Bay, 'Now for a monument in Westminster Abbey!'

We were cruising off Marittimo, with a combined squadron of eighteen sail of the line, for the defence of Sicily, menaced by a French fleet, with troops, lying in Vardo Bay near Genoa, and Lord Nelson would have sunk, with all his gallant fleet, before they could have effected a landing. His gratitude to the Neapolitan court was enthusiastic and unbounded, and he held life in light estimation compared with their welfare. Indeed, their munificent gifts, their admiration, I can almost say adoration, of our Norfolk hero, whose ship in their ports was always surrounded by their boats filled with Italians, while bands of music thundered forth, 'See the Conquering Hero comes,' and when he showed himself, shouts of applause rent the sky. In fact, their anxiety was of the same engrossing nature as the people of the West, to behold Bonaparte in Plymouth Sound; and he must have been more or less than human not to have felt elated at such demonstrations of affection.

'They never, Hardy, while I live shall pollute the soil of Sicily with their hateful presence,' said the Duke of Bronté and Nelson, as he quitted the deck to adorn himself with all his hard-won honours, which were to decorate his diminutive person on this gala day.

At last the sound of the 'Roast Beef of Old England' struck on my hearing and gladdened my heart, for I had shied my breakfast (not very inviting, by the bye), and shook the reefs out of my waist-coat to do honour to the noble lord's fare, who, with a fascinating smile, beckoned me, as being the youngest, to sit on his right hand, or where the right hand should have been if it had not been forcibly carried from its post by the Frenchman's ball. During the clatter of knives (for from their appetites most of the company, which was numerous, seemed to have imitated my example at the early meal of breakfast), Tom Allen's voice (which was far from musical, and rather forte than piano) addressed the captain of a dashing frigate, noted for not thinking small beer of himself.

'Captain Coffield, may I be so bold as to ax how Tom Smith is?'

Tom Smith was a foretopman of the dashing frigate which had joined us that day from a cruise. Captain Coffield dropped his knife and fork, and raised his eyeglass with a stare of astonishment at honest Tom, who, nothing daunted, repeated the question. Lord Nelson's indignation now found vent in words.

'Quit the cabin, Thomas Allen! I really must get rid of that impudent lubber. I have often threatened, but somehow he contrives to defeat my firm intentions – he is faithful, honest, and attached, with great shrewdness mixed with his simplicity, which is unbounded. He was badly wounded in the action we are assembled to commemorate, nursed me tenderly at Santa Cruz, and is a townsman. I mention these things, Captain Coffield, in palliation of his freedom, and shall be glad to take wine with you.'

The captain lowered his eyeglass, and raised his wineglass, while he bowed to the sunny smile that ofttimes irradiated the melancholy and rather homely visage of Lord Nelson. During the foregoing scene, I had persevered with great steadiness in my desperate attack on the savoury viands of the admiral's hospitable board; and he, most probably thinking a little liquid desirable for me, pushed towards me what he jocosely termed his own bottle – that is, it contained Bronté made from his own estate – and requested me to take wine with him. Drawing my breath with greater freedom than I had for the previous half-hour done, I ventured to look off my plate, and beheld the good-natured smile I have before described, and received the bow of the hero of a hundred battles, decorated in all the brilliancy of stars and medals. This was an epoch in my life, and I treasure the remembrance.

The cloth had disappeared, the chaplain had returned thanks, in which I cordially joined, for I really felt grateful for the best blow-out I had enjoyed for months. Though his lordship ate sparingly of the simplest fare, the splendid table he kept would have afforded gratification to the most fastidious gourmand, and at that period of my life I looked to quantity more than quality; so much so, that an eminent officer, now high in rank, desired his steward, whenever he was honoured by my company, to dress an additional joint. His lordship, after taking a bumper in honour of the glorious victory of the year ninety-seven, addressed me in a bland tone –

'You entered the service at a very early age, to have been in the action off St. Vincent?'

'Eleven years, my lord.'

'Much too young,' muttered his lordship.

At this moment, honest Tom Allen pushed in his bullet head, with an eager gaze at his master, and after a little consideration, approached the admiral.

'You will be ill if you takes any more wine.'

'You are perfectly right, Tom, and I thank you for the hint. Hardy, do the honours. And, gentlemen, excuse me for retiring, for my battered old hulk is very crazy – indeed, not sea-worthy.'

And the greatest naval hero of the day was led from his own table by his faithful and attached servant, after drinking five glasses of wine.

Upon the death of that hero, this excellent man drained the bitter cup of poverty to its very dregs and would have been consigned to Burnham Thorpe workhouse by his grateful country, had not a worthy philanthropist (with whose friendship I am honoured) rescued him from such degradation, by bringing his hard case to the knowledge of that great and good man, the late Sir Thomas Hardy, who made him pewterer of Greenwich Hospital, from which comfortable situation death removed him in a very summary manner, leaving his old dame a burthen on the finances of the friends of my most humane and excellent friend, who had formerly preserved them from the cold comforts of a workhouse. The Father of all will reward him.

A scene which displays the almost infantine simplicity of Tom Allen's mind occurs now to mine, nor am I aware, without looking over my Nelsonians, if I have before related it. When the King of Naples, of that day, joined his Majesty's ship *Foudroyant* in his own Bay of Naples, being afraid to land in his own capital, which was convulsed and torn to pieces by political rancour, and saturated with blood by those hell-hounds that disgrace the human form, and were embodied under the Lord Primate, Cardinal Ruffo, by the derisive title of the Christian Army – when he stepped from his own frigate, on our quarter-deck, Lord Nelson, with the officers of seventeen British ships of the line, were assembled in full fig to receive him; we were likewise crowded with ambassadors and ambassadresses, generals, princes, and potentates. The king was a good-looking man, of middle age and healthy appearance, and with great good-nature gave his hand to be kissed, by any person who fancied such absurd custom an honour. Among the rest our worthy Tom Allen received it with the unmeaning English salutation of 'How do you do, Mishster Allen?' delivered in jargon between Italian and English. Mishster Allen, as the king called him, gave the said hand a squeeze that appeared to me to convey to its royal owner anything but pleasure, with a truly Norfolk shake, that I thought likely to effect a dislocation of that useful member from the shoulder, and a coarse growl of 'I hope you are well, Muster King. How do you do, Muster King?' This Norfolk mode of salutation created astonishment in the king and courtiers, anger in Lord Nelson, and great mirth in Lady Hamilton and her fair *coterie*, who, approaching honest Tom, tried to persuade him to kneel down and ask permission to kiss his Majesty's hand; but Tom gruffly declared he never bent his knee but in prayer, and he feared that was too seldom.

When under fire from the forts of Valletta, which hulled the ship, and knocked away our foretopmast, this faithful servant interposed his bulky form between those forts and his little master, who was in a towering rage with his nephew, Sir William Bolton, for allowing her to drift into such a dangerous position. This affectionate domestic watched his lordship with unceasing attention, and many times have I seen him persuade the admiral to retire from a wet deck, or a stormy sea, to his bed. Like Lady Hamilton, however, upon the death of the heroic Nelson, he was consigned to oblivion and miserable poverty.

> 'Behold him stalk along the pier,
> Pale, meagre, and dejected,
> View him begging for relief,

And see him disregarded;
Then view the anguish in his eye –
And say our Tar's rewarded.'

Peace to the *manes* of honest Tom Allen!

'For though his body's under hatches,
His soul is gone aloft.'

Old songs by Dibdin, who likewise passed his age in miserable poverty.

Billy Culver

This most eccentric being prided himself on being the oldest midshipman in the Royal Navy, which he thought preferable, by great odds, to the youngest lieutenant. He was well connected, and a nephew of Lord Hood's, who once undertook the liquidation of his debts.

'I am amazed, Mr. Culver, really lost in astonishment, at the extreme length' – unfolding a bill equal to the proctor's displayed by Lord Cochrane in the House of Commons – 'and at the items of this extraordinary bill; to grog, one shilling; to ditto, ditto, ditto: there seems nothing but suction; not a meal mentioned.'

'Why, my lord, some people like eating, and often kill themselves by gluttony; I prefer drinking, and avoid such a catastrophe.' Lord Hood smiled, and paid the bill.

During his lordship's presiding over the Admiralty, Mr. Culver made his appearance, in obedience to an order of their lordships, issued a calendar month back.

'Before Sir Evan Nepean can see you, sir, he desires to know, through me, why you have so long delayed complying with their lordships' order?'

This interrogatory from the Admiralty messenger threw a thoughtful shade over Billy's open brow; and, after a slight consideration, he replied: 'I got under weigh the very instant I could command a clean shirt to appear before their lordships in, and cruised in a lubberly leathern convenience, drawn by four half-starved horses. I kept the quarter-deck, with a good look-out ahead, and at times conned the consarn by desiring coachee to starboard, or port, as occasion required. At the half-way house, he shortened sail, and hove-to, and ordered a glass of grog; this made me call for two, or perhaps three, and I remained in the same house till the day previous to yesterday; when, finding the tide ebbing fast out of my money-locker, at nearly low water I again got under weigh, and made all the sail I could carry for the Admiralty, and here I am.'

'You are a rum one,' said the messenger, 'but a shorter yarn must be given to Sir Evan.'

'Why, then, if it must be concise, say I was drunk.'

'If I do, your commission as lieutenant will be cancelled. Be advised by me, and say you were taken very ill on the road; and we must cook up a sick certificate.'

'What!' said Billy, looking sternly at him; 'tell a lie, a cowardly lie, at my time of life? Look you, sir! as man or boy, I never wilfully told a lie, and at the age of fifty it is too late to begin. Tell him I was drunk.' And Billy returned to the *Royal William* at Spithead, still the oldest midshipman in His Majesty's service.

On my alighting from the heavy coach, early in the year 1795, at the India Arms, Gosport, the first person who noticed me was this most eccentric midshipman; he was seated on a low settle by the large kitchen fire of that respectable house, with an outsized rummer of darkish liquor.

'What cheer, young squeaker? and what ship are you bound for?'

'The *Barfleur*, sir.'

'Do you like grog?'

'I don't know, sir; for I never tasted it.'

'Here, then,' said he, kindly getting off the settle, and putting it to my lips; 'take a swig, and let me know if it is stiff enough. Old Mother does not make good nor'-westers this month, the last score not being paid up.'

All of this was lost on my comprehension, and the only thing I understood was, that I must give an opinion on its merits, and accordingly swallowed some with great difficulty, for to me it was nauseous.

Billy contemplated my wry faces and aversion with astonishment and indignation. 'You must alter very materially to make a sailor, young squeaker.' And he resumed his seat on the settle, where, I am told, a gentleman once left him basting a roasting goose, with a glass of grog beside him; made a voyage to the East Indies, came back, and found Billy in the same place, employed in the same manner.

Billy Culver, to the best of my recollection, was a short, thick-set man, with rotundity of body, and a red, well-pimpled, or grog-blossom face; and long, long ago, might invariably have been found on the settle, by the kitchen fire of the India Arms, Gosport, busily employed in superintending bird or beast, revolving on the old-fashioned spit; and if it required basting, Billy was nothing averse to perform that part of the culinary duty.

A greenhorn of a lieutenant, who had recently been entered for provisions on board the *Royal William*, as supernumerary waiting for a passage to the West Indies, at one p.m. disagreeably surprised Billy in his usual avocation of basting a fine goose. As the day was warm, Billy sat without his coat, his shirt-sleeves tucked up, and an over-sized ladle in his hands.

'Mr. Culver, I presume?' said Greenhorn.

'I am called Billy Culver,' said our friend, removing the little three-cornered hat from his capacious cocoa-nut.

'I am extremely sorry to announce to you, Mr. Culver' –

'Billy, if you please, sir.'

'Well, then, if it will soften the unpleasant information, Mr. William Culver' –

'I answer to no other name but Billy Culver,' replied our old friend; 'but I see you are heated, sir; try a swig out of my rummer' – and he presented his large glass, with the reddish liquor, to the young officer, who thankfully drank till Billy called 'Belay there'; and the officer, after drawing breath, in a courteous manner said –

'It is my unpleasant duty to arrest you, as absent without leave, and convey you, as a prisoner, on board the *Royal William* guard-ship.'

'This is very *mal à propos*, as I was to dine with some friends on the fine bird before you; but I will put on my coat and attend you to old Grimsby, who is very harsh, as I am only a few days over my leave of absence granted by him. May I beg the favour of you not to let it burn till I can send the cook in?' So saying, Billy slipped on his coat, and slipped out of the back-door, and very soon reported himself as come on board, to first Lieutenant Grimsby.

'Mr. Culver, you have overstayed your time three days, and I have sent Lieutenant Greenhorn to bring you off under an arrest. Have you seen him?'

'Dear me, how strange!' said Billy, endeavouring to look very innocent; 'after taking our nooner together (by this he meant a glass of grog, a bad custom in vogue among seamen, even in these days of refinement and reform), I left him in full uniform, basting a goose roasting by the kitchen fire of the India Arms, Gosport; and if you will please to allow me to fulfil an indispensable engagement this day, I will, on my passage, make known to him your commands.'

'Send him off instantly, sir; such conduct is particularly unbecoming in an officer or a gentleman.'

And our acquaintance, Lieutenant Greenhorn, was ever after facetiously termed Goose Gibbey. I believe Billy's objections to being the youngest lieutenant were in course of time conquered, and that he died in a rank I never expect to obtain, that of post-captain.

Sir Sidney Smith

This chivalrous Knight of the Sword has been removed, I trust, to a better world. I remember him well, and have him in 'my mind's eye,' as he stepped on the quarter-deck of H.M. frigate *El Carmen*, lying in Aboukir Bay, Egypt, in the latter part of the year 1801. He was then of middling stature, good-looking, with tremendous moustachioes, a pair of penetrating black eyes, an intelligent countenance, with a gentlemanly air, expressive of good nature and kindness of heart.

'Captain Selby,' said the hero of Acre, 'if you will do me the honour to be guided by my advice, we will make a passage that shall astonish the world.'

For we were ordered to England to announce our success over the French army in Egypt, which, by convention, were to be sent as prisoners of war to Toulon. And Captain Selby did follow Sir Sidney's advice, and did astonish the world – but it was by the length of time we took to accomplish the passage. A sloop of war, which sailed a fortnight after us with duplicates, arrived exactly that time before us; by which *contretemps* Captain Selby lost knighthood, and five hundred pounds, the usual reward of bearing such news as we were freighted with.

'It is not the lot of mortals to command success,' said Addison; but we did more in *El Carmen* – we endeavoured to deserve it; for, by the advice of Sir Sidney, we hugged the Barbary coast close, in hopes of receiving the land-wind at night. Alas! everything, as frequently is the case, turned out the reverse of our expectations; the land-wind disdained to fill our sails, but the lee-wind blew hard upon us, and nearly wrecked the old tub off Cape Dern. She was a Spanish frigate, captured and brought into the service in the late war with that afflicted country, the fairest portion of the globe, so long a prey to intestine divisions and external war. Their conduct to the aboriginal inhabitants of the southern continent of America has surely drawn down the vengeance of a God of justice, for their nefarious and bloodthirsty treatment of a mild race of inoffensive people, whose last heroic chief, stretched by these hell hounds on live coals, his patient suffering under torture, his magnanimous saying to his fellow-sufferer, ere his tongue, swelled with fervid heat, refused its power of utterance, 'Am I, then, on a bed of roses?' Who can contemplate these diabolical deeds, and wonder that they are so afflicted? 'Vengeance is mine, and I will repay, saith the Lord;' and behold, in them His words are fearfully fulfilled. Look at this once far-famed nation, not long back the first in rank and power, when the gallant Francis I. of France wrote, as their captive, from the field of Pavia, 'Madam, we have lost all but our honour;' or when their proud Armada swept the British Channel, and their gorgeous ensigns overshadowed the Union Jack, intending, by their thumb-screws and hellish devices, to bend our free necks to bigotry and slavery's chains. It was then Britain's hardy sons, and England's iron-bound coast, defeated, by the help of God, their ambitious project. But my feelings are running me off my course, and with this admonition, England, look to thine acts in India and Africa! I will return to my tale of what happened long, long ago. Behold this Spanish tub (age unknown), under close-reefed topsails, and reefed courses, going one foot ahead, and two feet to leeward – a thick haze – no observation for two days previous – wind blowing dead on shore – a sneezer and no mistake – first lieutenant fidgety – and with the gunner securing guns with hammocks, hawsers, and cleats; for the heaviness of the sea, made her roll gunnel-to, and great apprehensions were entertained of the bolts drawing, and setting our eighteen-pounders free, the consequence of which would be instant destruction.

Sir Sidney's good-humoured countenance acquired a more sedate cast, and Captain Selby gazed eagerly to leeward, and evinced great anxiety, for we only guessed at our situation, which, by our dead reckoning, was sufficiently near the horrible coast of Barbary to justify more apprehension than was openly displayed.

'Get a cast of the deep-sea lead, Mr. Mowbray,' said the captain, addressing Old Soundings, the master.

'Ay, ay, sir.'

'Men in the weather chains, and pass the line along; all ready, forward from the weather cathead; heave without shortening sail, Mr. Mowbray, for fear we have no room to spare; look at her wake.'

'She falls to leeward like a sand-barge, fifty fathoms up and down,' called the master, 'and no bottom.'

'Examine the arming, master,' said Sir Sidney; 'the ship labours much.'

'It has not struck bottom, Sir Sidney. I believe it a bold shore and an iron-bound coast, steep and inaccessible.'

'You were wrecked in a sloop commanded by the Hon. Courtney Boyle?'

'Yes, Sir Sidney, near Arab's Tower, a very different coast to the one directly to leeward.'

The short autumnal day was closing in; the sun was setting in the midst of heavy clouds, nearly obscured by mist, but casting a red and threatening farewell glance at us, who still plodded on, one foot ahead and two to leeward, pitching bows under, and nearly burying herself in water.

Soundings and myself had charge of the middle watch, though few got any sleep on this dreary, long night. I had nominal charge, Mr. Mowbray *de facto*; the captain did not think a boy quite competent, to the serious duty that might devolve on him, for making Cape Dern suddenly in such a sea as was then running. Ensconced under the weather bulwark, being tired of listening to the groaning and creaking timbers of the *El Carmen*, as she laboured and strained through the mountainous waves that frequently broke upon, and half filled the waist, added to these melodies the clanking of the chain pumps, gave every tone but a lively tenor.

'Mowbray,' said I, 'cheer me with a short yarn of your adventures among the Monsieurs, when wrecked with Captain Boyle.'

'Agreed, my boy; and as Sir Sidney and the captain have (tired of watching) gone down for their middle watchers, send the youngster to forage.'

This produced salt junk and a glass of grog, which animated Soundings sufficiently to begin his short yarn, after having again cautioned the lookout men to look well for the land to leeward; and, taking up a position in the topsail halliard rack, he commenced as follows:–

MOWBRAY'S YARN

'I think I have described our reaching the shore on rafts, and being saved from the tender mercies of the Bedouin Arabs by a French party of cavalry, who arrived very opportunely; I imagine you have heard me speak of these things.' 'One hundred times,' I was on the point of exclaiming, but checked myself, for the master's tale was a standing dish in our gunroom, and came with the wine on the dinner-table daily, the name of the Hon. Courtney Boyle always producing the following yarn.

'I have a recollection of having told you how hard we fared in Alexandria, even during the time of "Kleber"; but when that excellent general (the very best and most skilful Frenchman in Egypt) fell beneath the assassin's dagger, our treatment was abominably cruel. His successor, Menou, (whom many people suspected) chose to throw the suspicion on us, the English prisoners of war, and, to give publicity to his suspicions, placed us in a circle round the stake that the wretched youth was impaled on. Never, no, never, shall I forget the bloody and brutal sight! The French army formed three sides of a square near the palm trees on the desert side, and close to Alexandria; the open space was to allow the ingress of the Bedouin Arabs, who flocked in countless numbers to see their countryman die by the dreadful death of impalement. The drums beat to arms by daylight, and our ferocious guards urged our immediate march; we were then placed, with scoffs, jeers, insults, and curses, close around where the stake was intended to be planted immediately. The garrison had formed, on came the advanced guard, the prisoner, and the executioner bearing the stake. The misguided youth, clad in a loose frock, such as carters wear in England, and bareheaded, walked to the scene of his torments with a firm step, head elevated, and eyes expressive of a mind at peace, stored with undaunted courage; his guard now reversed arms, while the bands struck up a solemn dirge, and the youthful prisoner – for I do not think he had reached twenty-five years – was conducted into the centre of the square; the slight covering was removed – and a better proportioned, athletic youth never stripped; he was then forcibly thrown on his face, his hands and feet secured, and the stake, which was hard wood pointed with shoulders, driven by the executioner into his back-bone. A horrid yell of anguish announced the commencement of his sufferings. He was an enthusiast, and conceived his Koran advised him to be a murderer. Poor youth! he expiated such misconception by suffering torments that the ingenuity of the Indians could hardly equal. The wretched youth was then raised, and the stake placed in the socket of a shaft sunk deep in the sand, with his face and naked body turned to the sun, that fiercely glared upon him. Although protected by light clothing from its rays, I felt melting beneath its intense heat, greatly augmented by reflection from the white sand on which we stood. O God! it was a pitiable sight to see that manly form, in the image of his Maker, so borne up, the muscles and veins standing out like cords on his body, throat, and legs, while every nerve quivered with excessive anguish; but his face, that had expressed manly courage and resignation, now was flushed with agony; while the eyes, protruding from the sockets, looked up with supplication for aid, as he loudly invoked his prophet, intermingled with cries for water, water. To these dreadful heart-rending cries, we were compelled to listen, and our sight was shocked by the unutterable agony that convulsed his body, till the hour of noon, when we were marched back to our caravansary or prison – the crowd of Arabs driven out of the square – the troops dismissed to their quarters, leaving a strong guard round the victim of ferocious cruelty, who writhed upon his stake with undiminished power of suffering. That night I could not sleep, for his dreadful cries still rang in my ears. Again we had to march at daylight, and circle round the stake, where the wretched youth still retained life, with power to utter hollow groans that nearly congealed my blood; but when my sight beheld the effect on his manly form from that night of agonised suffering, I closed my eyes, nor would I open them again to be blasted by such a sight of horror. His eyes and lips had been torn away by birds of prey, who, disturbed at their banquet on his body, still wheeled in circles above our heads, uttering loud discordant screams, while clouds of insects were eating him alive.

'But hold on, lads,' shouted the master, 'for here comes a topper.'

The frigate, from having little way, had fallen off in the trough of the sea, and a mountainous wave rolling on the beam seemed determined to swamp us; onward it came in its resistless might, breaking over the frigate, and sweeping away the boats and spare spars.

'Hold on, good sticks,' said Sir Sidney, who, with the captain, being aroused by the concussion, came running on deck.

'Land three points on the lee-bow,' called the lee cathead-man.
'Wear the ship, Captain Selby,' advised Sir Sidney.

'It is Cape Dern,' said Sir Sidney, 'and I fear we are embayed. All hands wear ship, ahoy.'

After a shrill whistle from the boatswain and his mates, and 'tumble up there – tumble up,' sounded through the decks of the *El Carmen*, 'Take the mainsail in, Mr. Langden, weather clue first'; but although our first luff proceeded to shorten sail in a seaman-like manner, the mainsail blew to ribbons as she came to the wind on the other tack; and, fortunately for the old frigate, it so happened, for we were taken flat aback in a heavy squall, and, had the mainsail still remained set, we most certainly should have gathered stern way, and foundered, like the *Centaur* and prizes taken in that gallant action of the twelfth of April. There is a guiding hand in all these events, which are not left to chance – 'no Christian should mention the word,' he cannot believe in it. From forty-five years' experience at sea, I have no doubt of a particular Providence in all these escapes, and God help us, if it did not exist, the foresight of the cleverest seaman would avail but little; but

> 'There's a sweet little cherub that sits up aloft,
> To look out a good berth for poor Jack.'

In the preceding part, I have said very little of the hero of my tale; I now beg leave to introduce him to my readers as he appeared to me; no passer-by of observation, however hurried, but would stop to get a second glance of this heroic prince of chivalry, whose manners would have done honour to Lord Chesterfield's tuition, and whose heart was the seat of kindness, good humour, and hilarity. He was the life of the ship, composed songs, and sang them; full of anecdote, so well told that you lost sight of the little bit of egotism they smacked of.

'I have some knowledge of that man at your weather wheel,' said he to me one morning, as we paced the quarter-deck of His Majesty's frigate. 'In what ship have we sailed together, my man?'

'No ship, Sir Sidney; but your honour will recollect that bit of a scrimmage with Mounseer in Ancona?'

'I do perfectly recollect that I owe my life to the courage of you and your companions, and here is a guinea to impress it on your mind.' And Sir Sidney resumed his walk.

'At the time he alluded to, I commanded a frigate lying in the little port of Ancona – it was just previous to our declaration of

war – and in the midst of the French revolutionary fury, I gave a
dinner in their best hotel to the royalists, both ashore and afloat; and
in the height of our hilarity, the Jacobins of the town, headed by the
crew of a French privateer, madly intoxicated, surrounded the
house, for the purpose of exterminating the aristocrats. The chairs
and tables were converted into weapons of defence; as my uniform
sword was the only warlike instrument, and it rendered good service
by letting out the life's blood of two leaders of this sanguinary band;
but we were sore pressed and outnumbered, as three of my friends
had been torn to pieces by the infuriated mob, when, by God's good
providence the crews of the English ships lying in the port came to
our rescue, and barely in time to save me from dangling at the
window sill, through which they were forcing me with a hempen
cravat, more useful than ornamental, when the hearty British cheer
stopped their proceedings, and obliged them to use their legs as
their best mode of defence and only means of safety. I need not tell
you that my friend at the wheel behaved well at the rescue.'

Sir Sidney, who shortened his moustachioes daily, according to
our run made in the night, fully determined to get rid of them by
our arrival in England, was to me an object of great interest from
the anecdotes my messmate, Dick Janverin, who served under him
in the *Tigre* at the renowned defence of Acre, used to tell us. *À
propos* of my friend Dick, who merited and obtained a post-
captain's rank previous to his early and much-lamented death.
This officer, whose unequalled adventures I hope some day, by the
permission of his friends, to give the public in my reminiscences,
was despatched by Sir Sidney at Acre, to give his Sublime
Highness at Constantinople, the interesting account of his defeat-
ing Bonaparte, at the head of his conquering legions, by the simple
aid of a British seventy-four and his own great skill. Captain
Janverin travelled through the desert with no other protection
than an Arab guide, his own strong arm, and dauntless heart. He
was overwhelmed on the passage, by the sands of the desert, raised
into mountains by the awful simoon, or fiery wind, extricated and
tenderly nursed by the Bedouin Arabs, who are ever roaming its
pathless track, and conducted by them safely through its solitary
waste. But I perceive the name of my friend Janverin has caused
me, in nautical language, to take a broad yaw; therefore, to return
to the hero of my tale, who, Janverin used to tell us, was the best

runner he ever met with, for when reconnoitring the French army before Acre, his companions would point out to Sir Sidney, that the sharp-shooters had been thrown forward with a great wish to make him their target, for the defence of Syria and Acre depended on his life.

'I see them lying down under the ridges of sand in front, Sir Sidney, and they will put a ball through you before you can say Jack Robinson.'

'Now, boys, the devil take the hindmost!' and Sir Sidney would enter the breach in the walls, where Jezza Pacha made his bed every night during the siege, before his companions were half way. In course of time, but long over due, we made Gibraltar, and there landed General Sir Edward Paget, and several military officers, who were heartily tired of us. On our passage down, we one night fell in with a frigate, and, taking her for an enemy, from not answering our signals, prepared for action, when Sir Sidney appeared on deck in the costume of Robinson Crusoe, a rifle on each shoulder, and countless pistols.

'I will head the boarders, Captain Selby, and only advise one broadside, with the muzzle of your guns touching the Frenchman's.'

But the Frenchman turned out to be an Algerine frigate, and Sir Sidney detained her two hours, while he wrote instructions to the Bey of Dern, should the French again attempt a landing on his frowning coast, and among his savage subjects, to whom we had the pleasant prospect of becoming hewers of wood and drawers of water, if we escaped the impending shipwreck, which the sudden shift of wind so providentially saved us from, when embayed on that dangerous coast. Taking in fresh water, and landing some nobs of passengers, among which was the before-named general, who was without exception a most finished gentleman and an excellent officer. I think I read of his death a few days back, and grieve much that such ornaments to society should grow old and die off like the common clods of this earth, who is many instances vegetate like cabbages, and die unloved and unknown, superior to the brute creation only in speech, which gift is too often abused by blasphemous oaths and dreadful revilings; but a truce to moralising – a few hours again saw us through the straits, and in the vast Atlantic. Sir Sidney, among many peculiar eccentricities, asserted that rats fed cleaner, and were better eating, than pigs or ducks; and, agreeably to his wish, a dish of these beautiful vermin were caught daily with fish-hooks, well baited, in the provision hold, for the ship was infested with them, and served up at the captain's table; the sight of them alone, took off the keen edge of my appetite. Some days previous to striking soundings, it blew so hard, with such a sea, as was conceived dangerous for the old tub to scud in; accordingly she was made snug by getting the top-gallant masts on deck, and we hove-to under a close-reefed main-topsail. I only saw Sir Sidney once during the gale, when he jocosely remarked that he was only a passenger, and therefore should return to his cot, which he deemed the most comfortable place in the ship. On the following morning, the wind having moderated, we bore up, and shook a reef out of the topsails, dropped the foresail, and stood under the stern of a large ship, labouring heavily with top-gallant yards across in a topping sea, and American colours reversed.

'I am in a sinking state,' said brother Jonathan, 'and I calculate I shall only be able to keep her up two hours or so; the people are frightened, and I am in a bit of a shake; therefore, Britisher, I will take it as a compliment if you will send your boat (mine are washed away), and save us from being drowned like rats, in this tarnation leaky hooker.'

'I will stay by you,' said Captain Selby, 'but no boat will live in this sea.'

Upon this declaration, Jonathan Corncob spat twice as fast as ever, and observed, 'You might oblige us with a boat, captain?'

His passengers and crew did not take it in the same cool way their master did, but raised a great outcry, and threw up their hands to a superior power for aid; while despairingly they tried to induce us to send a boat. Sir Sidney's kind heart was touched by the scene.

'Captain Selby, if you will risk your lee-quarter cutter, I will save, by the help of Heaven, those despairing creatures. Give me choice men, good boatmen, Mr. Langdon, and, with your captain's permission, I will take you in the boat.'

This speech relieved me from a heavy weight of care, for, as officer of the watch, it was my duty to share the risk with Sir Sidney; but I had not the slightest inclination to be drowned, even in such good company, and his choice fell on the first lieutenant (there is no accounting for taste); it set both heart and mind at rest; for I fully concurred with my captain in opinion that no boat could live.

Sir Sidney was the first man to spring into the lee-cutter. Captain Selby having remonstrated against his risking so valuable a life, was answered gaily by the gallant hero calling to our first luff, 'Mr. Langdon, if your tackle-falls give way, you will be drowned for your carelessness, as I intend to be lowered in the boat, and her tackle-falls should always be ready to bear any weight. Now for a bow and stern fast well attended, and your two best quarter-masters at the falls. Watch her roll, men, when I give the word, for on your attention and skill depend the lives of the cutter's crew, your first luff, to say nothing of my own, and Chips, the carpenter, whom, with your leave, Captain Selby, I will take on board Jonathan, who I suspect is not so bad as stated, but rather lost in his reckoning. Additional stretchers in the boat, Mr. Langdon; each man with them in his hands to bear us off the side. Now, Captain Selby, place your frigate close on her weather-quarter, to make a lee for us.' And every man held his breath with consternation, as the gallant hero, watching the lee roll, loudly gave the word to lower away roundly – still louder, to let go and unhook, on the celerity of which depended all their lives. I drew my breath freely, when the boat showed her stern to the mountainous waves, impelled by her oars, as each billow threatened to engulf her, and the cool magnanimity of Sir Sidney, as he steered alongside the wall-sided monster of a Yankee, who rolled awfully as he sprang on board.

'I guess you are the captain of that there Britisher,' said Jonathan Corncob, addressing the hero of Acre; 'and I take your conduct as most particularly civil.'

'I am only a passenger in yon frigate, and am called Sir Sidney Smith; but let your carpenter show mine where he thinks the leak is, and I shall be glad to look at your chart.'

'You shall see it, Sidney Smith (we do not acknowledge titles in our free country);' – and Jonathan unrolled a very greasy chart before Sir Sidney.

'I do not see any track pricked off. What was your longitude at noon yesterday? and what do you think your drift has been since that time?'

'Why, to tell you the truth, Sidney Smith, I 'av'n't begun to reckon yet; but mate and I was about it when the gale came on. I think we are about here.' And Jonathan Corncob covered many degrees with the broad palm of his hand. 'Mate thinks we are more to the eastward.'

This convinced Sir Sidney, that he rightly guessed, that the man was lost. Americans, long, long ago, were not pre-eminent as now in navigation, and were generally and irreverently called God's ships. The carpenter, by this time, had diminished the leak; and Sir Sidney, giving Captain Corncob the bearings and distance of Brest, only a day's sail dead to leeward, offered to take him and his crew on board the *El Carmen*, leaving the boat's crew to run the tarnation leaky hooker into Brest, and claiming half her value as salvage.

But Jonathan gravely demurred, and calling to mate, 'Reverse our stripes, and place our stars uppermost again, where they should be,' while he kindly slapped Sir Sidney on the shoulder, calling him an honest fellow from the old country; and in the fulness of his gratitude offered him a quid of tobacco and a glass of brandy.

Sir Sidney got on board without accident, and Jonathan Corncob made all sail for Brest, where I trust (but never heard) that he safely arrived.

The following letter from Sir Sidney to Captain Janverin, who sought employment in the Austrian service, will show the amiability and kindness of his excellent heart. And allow me to introduce my old messmate, Dick Janverin, who died at an early age in France, where he had resided on a post-captain's half-pay, having received various wounds, and encountered many hair-breadth escapes, that would have destroyed any other constitution and frame; but his were, like his nerves, firm as iron and true as steel. I have him now in my mind's eye, as with his herculean frame he stood modestly uncovered before Lord Nelson on the quarter-deck of the flagship, the *Foudroyant*, in Palermo Bay. The case was, a number of wild midshipmen played so many mad pranks on the previous night at the Opera House, that the audience with one consent united to turn them out; this was strenuously resisted; but, considerably outnumbered, and sight dazzled by that effective bright, but small instrument, the stiletto, a retreat was ordered by our commander Janverin, who covered our rear, by levelling the Italians with his powerful fists, and few possessed so much power;

they fell before him like corn before the reaper; so that we effected our escape to the Spanish coffee-house, and, gathering the British midshipmen there assembled, loaded several coaches, and returned to the attack; but the manager had most wisely closed the house, and we were now called by Lord Nelson to rebut the chief justice's charge of having created a riot. Janverin was our spokesman, and assured his lordship we had only acted in self-defence, and received even blows before we thought of returning them.

'Mr. Janverin,' said Lord Nelson, 'you have more the appearance of the lion than the lamb, and I prohibit any petty officers from going on shore, except on duty.'

Our leave was stopped till the capture of the *Guillaume Tell* again restored it. Dick Janverin left us, to join his old friend and captain, Sir Sidney Smith, and I now proceed to give part of his eventful life in his own simple and modest narrative.

'RICHARD GAVE JANVERIN, ESQ., LATE POST-CAPTAIN IN HER MAJESTY'S FLEET

'Paris, 15 April 1818

'My DEAR SIR, – I do not lose a post, having an opportunity clear of the foreign mails, and knowing your precise address from your last letter, to acknowledge it, and to say I agree with you in your reasoning, now that Austria and we have avowedly the same interests, though it was a delicate ground to touch, whilst the state of Italy and France was unsettled, and she liable to be forced to make unwilling and distressing sacrifices, as heretofore, for the sake of peace and political existence.

'I shall be most happy to further your views, under my experience of your indefatigable zeal and nautical knowledge, my conviction of your capacity to realise them with great credit to yourself and those who patronise you; among the latter you are right in reckoning on me.

'Now for the mode of proceeding. You must first become sufficiently master of the Italian language to enable you to command those who speak that only. Prince Nugent, with whom I can interest myself in your favour, speaks English fluently. I can get him to present you properly to those I am not in any degree of intimacy sufficient to take such a liberty with, as he knows them all; but we cannot, and must not presuppose that the Austrian government, though it may see its interests in a nautical establishment, feels or can be made to feel it sufficiently to make pecuniary sacrifices, or to withdraw a sufficient portion of its finance from the army, to create and support such an establishment.

'The application for you to be allowed to serve in a foreign state must be made by that government to ours; that *sine quâ non* was pointed out by the Admiralty, in answer to Wright's application for leave to serve in the Sardinian incipient navy.

'This not succeeding in Austria, you might get leave to create and command a Tuscan flotilla, that state being at war with the Barbaresques, through Austria not being covered from depredations by treaty with the Porte.

'I recommend your studying the Italian in Tuscany, and taking Prince Nugent's advice as to further proceedings. I am ready to answer any reference that Count Meerfeldt may make, in such manner as he will consider sufficiently favourable to authorise his recommendation of you.

'Yours ever, with sincere esteem and regard,

'W. SIDNEY SMITH.'

CAPTAIN JANVERIN'S NARRATIVE

I went to sea in the *Resistance*, 44, Captain Edmund Pakenham, on the 5th of September 1793, being then near thirteen years old, having been born 2nd December 1780. I received a regular education at different schools, being intended for a mercantile life; but I ran from that situation, and was the founder of my own fortune in the navy, having entered as a boy. On the 19th of November 1793, we sailed for India, and the first shot I ever saw fired was in an action off the Mauritius, with the *Dugauez Firman*, a vessel which had formerly been the *Princess Royal*, Indiaman, had been captured early in the war, and fitted as a privateer. In this ship I was present at the capture of Malacca and its dependencies, and in 1796 at the capture of the Moluccas, and was employed with the small-arm men whenever their services were required, though without much real service, except in the beginning of 1797 and latter end of 1796, when I was in some smart bush-fighting with the revolted Malays.

In 1797, I was present at the attack of Copang, headed the parties in the destruction of this place, and was severely wounded in three places. During the time we were lying at Banda in this ship, the revolted slaves set fire to the town; and here I had the pleasure of preserving and restoring to their mother, at the imminent hazard of my own life (from a house that was in flames, and which was supposed to contain a quantity of gunpowder), two children, one the age of three years, and the other three months.

I quitted this ship at Amboyna, in October 1798, to join a ship, to which I had been appointed by Lord Keith, as a lieutenant, and at a very considerable expense to myself; for living on shore until a conveyance could be found, paying my own passage, etc. etc., cost me three hundred pounds before my arrival at the Cape; and there I had the mortification to find that the *Dordrecht*, to which I had been apppointed, had sailed for England. I now fully determined to quit the naval service, as, upon application to Sir Hugh Christian, then commander-in-chief of the navy, I could not get admittance on board any ship at that time in Table Bay, but was told I might pay my passage to England, if I wished to be there. I was thus thrown off from the service, after having served near five years, with some credit to myself, and having received some wounds in it.

This was the second disappointment; the first had originated with Captain Pakenham refusing to allow me a passage to China, to which place he was going, though I requested and urged it very frequently in a correspondence which passed. The only reason I could elicit from him for not allowing me a passage was, that the route to China was not that of the Cape of Good Hope, though at that time it appeared to be the only chance I had of being enabled to get a passage for that colony. I, however, succeeded afterwards in a ship, which had come as a transport from India, and which, fortunately for me, was ordered to the Cape. Had it not been for the humanity of Mr. Jones, the Company's agent at Amboyna, I should probably have starved at that place, as, when Captain Pakenham sent me on shore from the *Resistance*, I had but five Spanish dollars to maintain myself till I could get a passage, and to pay for such passage, a distance of five or six thousand miles. However, I suppose this was considered to be for the good of the service. Mr. Jones took my word and my bill, and supplied me with money, for which I shall always feel grateful, and promised, if no other opportunity offered, that he would order me a passage in a ship of the Company's, which had arrived to land spices. Out of evil cometh good. Had I gone in the *Resistance*, it is probable I should have lost my life, as that ship was blown up, and all hands perished. Having determined to quit the service, I had engaged with a Mr. Brown, then agent victualler at the Cape, to take command of a ship of his to India. This arrangement was concluded, when, to my astonishment, I received a letter from Sir Hugh Christian, to attend him, when he proposed my going home in a vessel, which he had purchased for the purpose of sending home despatches. This I refused, and was given to understand, if I did not comply, I should be treated as a deserter from the service. I had been living on shore at the Cape for a month, at no small expense; the despatches were intercepted ones from the French Directory to the governor of the Isle of France, apprising him of the expedition from Toulon. Here I again felt the strong hand of power; but it saved me a second time. The vessel I was to have commanded was taken by her crew of Malays, and all the officers were murdered. In this vessel, called the *Cornwallis*, commanded by Captain Byron, I embarked compulsorily for a second time in the naval service of my country, and, without any material occurrence, was paid off from her at Deptford in July 1798, and immediately joined the *Tigre*, then commanded by Sir Sidney Smith, and was with him during the siege of Saint Jean d'Acre, or at least arrived in time to see the commencement of it, as I had been put by him into the command of a small vessel purchased for the conveyance of despatches, and in which I escaped from a French squadron of three frigates and three brigs off Alexandria, and arrived in the Bay of Acre on the 19th of March, the day Bonaparte invaded that town. I had here a narrow escape, as I had anchored under Caiffa, not knowing that it was in the possession of the French, and had proposed to go on shore for intelligence of where Sir Sidney might be, when it came on to blow, and the next morning I found the French colours flying there. I was wounded in three places at the siege, severely.

After the defeat of Bonaparte, in the year 1799, before Acre, not having the means of conveyance for his sick and wounded by land, he was reduced to the necessity of relying on the justice of his conqueror for the freedom of a passage by water for part of them, and to his humanity for supplying them with provisions and necessaries, of which they were wholly destitute. This appeared rather an act of providential favour to Sir Sidney Smith, whose humanity had been called in question by Bonaparte, who had not scrupled to affirm he had enticed the French soldiers to desert, and had afterwards put them on board vessels infected with the plague for a conveyance to Toulon; thus fulfilling the promises held out to them. The absurdity of this charge would not require a refutation, if the world would give themselves a moment's time for consideration; as, however desirous Sir Sidney might have been to get clear of the French army, he never would have exposed a part of his own ship's company to the danger of infection, as it was necessary that men and officers should be sent to navigate the vessels. But to proceed.

On the afternoon of the 24th of May 1799, as the *Tigre* was proceeding down the coast of Palestine, a sail was discovered, which, on being boarded, proved to be a Turkish vessel, having on board two hundred and fifty wounded officers and men belonging to the French army, that had been sent from Jaffa in this vessel, without medicine, and almost destitute of provisions. The following is a copy of a letter written to Sir Sidney on this occasion:–

'On this application, myself[1] and seven men were sent from the *Tigre* to navigate the vessel to Damietta, and we were amply supplied with every requisite for dressing their wounds, by the surgeon, and with every comfort from Sir Sidney Smith's private stock. On the second day after quitting the *Tigre*, the vessel was wrecked on the desert of Syria, to the southward of El Arish, about the pitch of Kan, in a heavy gale of wind. I was then labouring under the pain of a still unclosed rifle wound through the right shoulder, but made every exertion to save the people, and at last happily accomplished it after great difficulty, remaining on board till every person was landed, the sea making a fair breach over the vessel, and expecting to part every moment. When the last party was landed, by some mismanagement of the seamen, in not attending to the swifter on the hawser, the boat was swamped on the beach; thus the little store of water that it might have been practicable to carry, was not available, and we found ourselves, without

---

[1] Mr. Janverin, master's mate.

victuals or drink, in the midst of a desert, and, as we believed, upwards of seventy miles from the nearest French post. To attempt returning was not to be thought of, certain destruction awaiting us from the Arabs if we had attempted it.

'Reduced to the necessity of trusting to the strength of a single arm in swimming through the breakers, I jumped overboard, and happily accomplished it, reaching the shore almost exhausted and expiring. A consultation was now held of what would be best to be done; and it was resolved to attempt reaching some of the frontier fortresses between the Nile and Syria. Our intention was, Tinch, if possible, and on calculating the supposed distance, it was found to be upwards of seventy miles. Those whose wounds were so severe as to prevent their moving, we were reduced to the necessity of leaving on the beach (to the mercy of that Providence who seldom forsakes his creatures in their distress) in the hope that some vessel passing down might be able to relieve them from their impending fate, or that the weather might prove so moderate that provisions might be procured from the ship; for which purpose, two of the seven men sent from the *Tigre* were left with them, from their own choice, rather than undergo the hardships and fatigue of endeavouring to find their way through the desert.

'After having arranged everything that could be done, we commenced our march at six o'clock in the evening of the 26th of May, carrying on our shoulders one of the French officers, who had been severely wounded, hoping to be able to keep him with us. We travelled in this way until about ten o'clock, when he desired to be left under some small shrubs (the only ones that we found for nearly two days), requesting, if any of us arrived at a French station, that we would despatch people to seek him, and, in case of his death, to bury him in the desert. I had with me a bottle of wine, which I secured about me when I jumped overboard from the wreck; this I gave him; and after taking leave, doubtful whose situation was the most desirable, we pursued our journey until daylight of the 27th, when, finding ourselves fatigued, we halted on the margin of the sea, which was still running dreadfully high. Here three of the remaining English returned to the wreck, alleging that, rather than suffer the fatigue that we had apparently to undergo, they would take their chance with the wounded left on the beach.

'After halting about four hours, we proceeded on our march, under all the influence of a vertical sun in these low latitudes, in the hottest time of the year. About mid-day we halted again, having proceeded, by our calculation, about thirty miles from the wreck. Here those who could do it, finding an excessive thirst, determined on bathing, that the pores might imbibe the moisture. Of this rash determination we heartily repented, as the particles of salt, which was formed upon the body after bathing, had such an effect from the friction of the clothes, as gave the skin the appearance of beef which had been salted, and we were obliged to shift off every article of clothing, except shirts and shoes, and travel in this manner. At sunset, again we halted for the night, much fatigued, and faint for want of sustenance, not having eaten or drunk anything since our departure from the wreck on the evening before.

'We now amounted to no more than one hundred and twenty, the rest having remained behind from fatigue, or returned to take their chance by the wreck. It was now quite calm, and my advice was that we should all return, as we had not yet completed more than half our computed distance; but, on revising our calculation, we found that instead of seventy miles, which we at first calculated, the distance was more than ninety, of which we had not completed more than forty. Yet scarcely a complaint was heard. About two in the morning of the 28th of May, we resumed our march, suffering all the horrors of thirty hours' deprivation from water. We kept along the seashore the whole of this day, till about four in the afternoon, when a French sergeant recognised a parcel of bricks, which he affirmed he had seen the year before, in visiting with Bonaparte the French posts on the confines of Syria, and that our distance from the French port of El Calich did not exceed twenty-five miles.

'This was joyful news to those who had been near forty-eight hours without sustenance of any kind. But, fearful of trusting to the knowledge of one man, which, should it not be correct, would involve us all in irremediable destruction, we determined to put it to the vote, which was in the affirmative. In fact, it appeared the lightest of two evils; it was becoming apparent that few if any of us would have strength sufficient to overcome the difficulties of fifty miles, which we calculated with some certainty yet remained for us to perform to the nearest French post, on the Lake of Mangala. With some faint hopes, but heavy hearts, we then committed ourselves to the deserts, and proceeded, by what we willingly believed had been a beaten track, until sunset, when we halted, having proceeded about two leagues into the desert. At this time we were so exhausted as to make it doubtful if any of us would again be able to rise. I now attempted to drink my own urine, but found it so bitter and unpalatable, that I was forced to desist. Not being able to sleep, I wandered about with the French sergeant, who had been guide, in hopes of finding some palm trees, which he said he had seen near the spot where we had halted. About twelve at night, we, by the help of the moon, discovered them, to our inexpressible satisfaction; as, wherever the palm tree is found, water, either good or bad, is certain. With an old cutlass we contrived to make an excavation, and found – oh, heavens, what were our feeling! – water, after having been deprived of it near fifty-four hours. Those who have felt the want of water, even in England, for ever so short a time, may judge what were our sensations, who had been so long deprived of it under a vertical sun, and had travelled during that time fifty-four miles. But our joy was considerably damped on finding it so nauseously bitter, that it required almost as great incentives as we were then labouring under, to induce us to drink of it. It allayed our thirst for the time, but the sensation left on the palate was, if possible, worse than the raging thirst. All, however, drank of it, and felt some refreshment, but none could be induced to try a second draught, and in a very short time the effects were felt, the water being strongly impregnated with salt.

'At daylight we again moved forward, and found that the road we had taken was a beaten track. At sunrise we were tantalised by the appearance of a lake of water. This extraordinary phantom, known by the appellation of 'mirage,' is occasioned by the dew that falls copiously during the night, being absorbed or drawn up by the power of the sun in half an hour after its rising; and although we were firmly persuaded, and, in fact, had certain knowledge, that no water could be there, still we followed the deception; and what is still more strange, disappointment was strongly expressed in the countenance.

'About ten o'clock we got sight of some trees, which our guide, to our no small joy, recognised. Here we again dug for water; but, though a height of four hundred feet above the level, at the depth of not more than two we found the water as salt as if it had been taken from the ocean. Having now reached a frequented country, it became necessary to make some appearance of a regular march, to intimidate the strolling parties of Arabs, should there be any on this track. Mustering our forces, we found only ninety-six of our original number. These we divided. Those best able were thrown out upon the flanks, carrying on their shoulders branches of palm trees divested of their leaves, which gave them at a distance an appearance of being armed. The others, were formed in marching order, and armed in the same manner. We had now been sixty-six hours without sustenance of any description, except the water got at the palm trees the second night of our journey. When ascending one of the numerous sandhills, about six o'clock, we got sight of the fortress of Calich, and in less than an hour were reconnoitred by the cavalry sent out for that purpose; an instant request was the consequence, for water and provisions, and a convoy of camels to pick up the stragglers. We arrived at the fortress at three o'clock, having been three days, wanting two hours, without refreshment, and the thermometer at Calich had not been, during that time, less than one hundred and five.

'It will not, I hope, be deemed presumptuous to give an opinion, in this place, as to the supposed contagious nature of plague. There does not remain a doubt of its having existed on board the squadron, consisting of the *Tigre*, eighty, Captain Sir Sidney Smith; *Theseus*, seventy-four, Captain R. W. Miller; and *Alliance*, store ship, Captain Wilmot; but in no instance was it found to be communicated from mere contact alone, from this proof:– When I had returned to Sir Sidney, and had the command of a squadron of gunboats, on going on shore at Jaffa, I found seven unfortunate Frenchmen in the act of being led from their hospital, where they had been left by the army, under plague, to be put to a summary death; and after a great deal of trouble (with an armed boat's crew) and some little danger from the Turkish soldiers, I rescued them, and took them on board the *Negress* with me, where they remained with the glandular swellings in a state of suppuration, and with only common precaution, for upwards of six weeks, when they were all landed at Damietta, and given up to the French army. No appearance of the plague ever existed on board the *Negress*, among a crew of twenty-eight men, besides officers. Another instance I would mention at Acre. When I was there, repairing a squadron of gun-vessels, it was reported that the Pacha's head gardener was ill of the plague. I went to his house, and found him utterly deserted by everybody but his wife. I kept in the house, performed the last offices of religion and humanity for him, but escaped the plague. The only precaution I used, was never to visit him with an empty stomach, and I fully consider a small portion of brandy, taken before visiting the patient, a sufficient preservative. I was after-wards overland to the Red Sea with Admiral Blankett, and the plague was supposed to be in the army, or that part of it which came up with him. I had no bed with me, and an officer having died of fever, his bed was ordered to be destroyed. I begged it, and slept upon it that night, and for years after, without inconvenience. From these trials, I judge the plague not to be so contagious as is supposed. I afterwards, in an inland journey, passed through a country which had been nearly depopulated by the plague, and halted in the different villages where it raged, without being affected. I consider cleanliness as the great preventive. The Turks wash and bathe frequently, but put on the same linen and clothes.

'On my arrival at Calich, I found a French officer (or rather German), whose name was Broff, in command of the garrison. Here I experienced every attention that it was possible to bestow, and remained one night. The next morning arrived some officers from the advanced guard of the French army, then retreating from Syria, who strongly desired my being sent on to Damietta, by a convoy then preparing for the Nile, as they asserted that Bonaparte would detain me, should I be found at Calich on his arrival, and that, from the humour he was in, I should not be pleased with my treatment. It was well that I took their advice, as the sequel will prove. Bonaparte arrived there that day. Being impatient to push on to Cairo, he did not receive the reports, but left an aide-de-camp to bring them, on his arrival at Cairo. When the report was made to him, he became absolutely furious, and immediately despatched orders to supersede the commandant of Calich, and to General Almiraz, who commanded at Damietta, to prevent my departure, and send me on to Cairo. I had the parole of the officers for my safe conduct and return to Sir Sidney Smith in my pocket. It fortunately happened that a Turkish vessel had been taken with French wounded by the *Tigre* after my departure. This vessel, General Almiraz, according to the convention, sent back to Sir Sidney

Smith, and in her I took my departure after a four days' stay at
Damietta, during which time I received from General Almiraz
every attention and care, and he loaded my vessel, on his departure,
with provisions of all descriptions, for my passage back to Acre. I
parted from him with regret.

'On passing the fort at Lesbe, the batteries commenced firing
upon me, for the purpose of making me heave-to, and a boat was
despatched for the purpose of detaining me. Having some presentiment it was by the order of Bonaparte, I determined to pay no
attention to either the boat or the firing; and, having a fine breeze
and rapid current, I was soon out of the reach of shot.

'On the evening of the 9th of June 1799, finding it impossible to
reach Acre that night, I ran into a small bight apparently in the
land, but which subsequently proved to be the harbour of Cesarea.
We anchored here before sunset, and, having an inclination to see
some part of the immense ruins which presented themselves, I
jumped overboard, accompanied by John Bell, the coxswain of the
Tigre's black cutter, and a Greek named Georgi. Not having a boat,
in this attempt I had very nearly perished. I had on a shirt and
trousers; but finding the shirt held a great deal of water, I was
endeavouring to clear myself of it, but my right arm being still
weak from the effects of the recent wound, I could not support
myself with it, and the shirt slipping down on my legs, had totally
disabled me from any exertion. Georgi, however, soon came to my
assistance, and cleared the disaster. On our arrival upon the shore,
we found the place had been a hospital for the sick and wounded,
the horrid remains of which still presented itself in half-burned
huts, and corpses which had evidently been poisoned, and the atro-
cious deed attempted to be hid from human knowledge by the
effects of fire. It was not probable that any European should visit
the spot, but it appears the heinous offence was attempted to be
concealed from the eyes of the barbarous inhabitants, as being too
cruel an act to be tolerated even by the wild inhabitants of that
coast. When we had recovered our horror-stricken faculties, we
counted in one place alone, not more than six yards square, the
mutilated remains of thirty-two bodies; some had evidently
suffered amputation, but all bore the unequivocal marks of poison.
The bodies had evidently swelled, and, from the very light materials of which the huts were composed, had not suffered considerably

from the effects of fire. I should estimate the whole number at near three hundred men. I found besides twelve pieces of brass ordnance, which had been sunk to prevent its falling into the hands of the Turks or British. These guns were afterwards got up, and added to the strength of Acre.

'Bonaparte was exasperated at my escape, and issued an order that, if taken in any part of Egypt, I should be immediately hung without trial. I also landed with a flag of truce on the subject of sick and wounded – communicated with the General Almiraz from Tinch, and was very near being again decoyed into the power of Bonaparte. My stay on the coast was near a fortnight; and after my first communications, a messenger was sent to Cairo by the General on the subject of my despatches, and I was to land on that day week for an answer. I did so; but not finding it, the officer commanding at Tinch induced me to stay till the next morning, which I did; but the answer not having arrived, I determined to return on board. As I crossed the bar of the harbour, a squadron of camels were perceived moving down; this I supposed must be the answer expected. Still, I had some idea that all was not right, and having been more than twenty-four hours from my command, and above all, having distributed the *French Gazetteer* and proclamations of the Ottoman Porte, enticing the French army to desert, I did not think it safe to comply with a signal made to me to return to the shore, but lay off at a little distance. The impetuosity of the cavalry saved me; for, finding that I did not appear to approach the shore, they commenced a heavy fire from their carbines, which went over, through, and under the boat, happily without doing injury to any person. On this hint I pulled on board, and so saved my life.

'General Almiraz was superseded, and all the officers of the garrison at Damietta; this I found when I joined the French army under the command of General Kleber, at Salagha, with the treaty of El Arish. He introduced me to the General in this way: "*Almiraz, voilà votre ami.*" This produced the explanation. Bonaparte afterwards told Mr. Keith, who was Sir Sidney's secretary, and with him upon some diplomatic business at Alexandria, that he had denounced me in army orders, and that, should I be taken, there was no hope for me. Keith answered this in the following spirited way: "General, we have some prisoners in the *Tigre;* there are more than ten thousand in England; if you hurt a hair of Mr. Janverin's head, except in allowed warfare, they shall answer it." Bonaparte then laughed, and said, "His intention was to send me round the Cape of Good Hope, by way of giving me a long passage to join Sir Sidney, to whom he knew I was valuable." Thus ended the conversation.

'I remained with Sir Sidney in the command of detached vessels until July 1799, when I went down to Palermo, to Lord Nelson, for the purpose of passing for a lieutenant. From him, I received a commission to command my old vessel, the *Negress*, as a regular gun-vessel. I returned, and joined Sir Sidney in December. While employed in this vessel off Jaffa, and having the *Dangereux*, commanded by Mr. * * * *, with me, I learned that a Hydriot vessel, then in the Roads, had appropriated to her own use some brass ordnance, which I had received orders to get up. This vessel was armed with twenty-two twelve-pounders, and full of men – had been fitted out at the island of Idria. I went on board to demand the guns, when resistance was made. I, however, succeeded in recovering them, and liberating from the Turkish yoke, or rather the yoke of pirates – for such I found they afterwards were – ten Italians, whom they had taken out of a Neapolitan vessel (which they had destroyed) and detained as slaves. This vessel had a firman from the Grand Seignior, and was manned with two hundred men. My small force consisted of *Negress*, six guns and twenty-eight men, and *Dangereux*, four guns and eighteen men. Here my life was saved by one of the boat's crew, of the name of Hooker. A Turk had placed the muzzle of his rifle close to the back of my neck, and was in the act of firing, when knocked down by him. This fellow I took on shore, and gave up to the governor of Jaffa, who executed summary justice upon him.

'Upon joining Sir Sidney again, I was recommended to his notice for the purpose of going to India with despatches, announcing the treaty of El Arish, which was signed on the 29th of January 1800; and on the 30th of the same month, I left the Vizier's camp at El Arish, with General Dessaix, Monsieur Ponsilieu, D'Anzelot, Savary, and Rapp. This journey brought me acquainted with most of the superior officers who had been serving under Bonaparte in Italy. With this party I went to Calich, where we met the advanced guard of the French army, composed of two thousand men. We proceeded to * * * *, and joined General Kleber with the main army, consisting of eight thousand, from whence we went to Cairo. I remained there from the 8th to the 16th of February, and visited the Pyramids, the Nile, the ruins on the island of Rhoda, and all the antiquities in the vicinity.

'Breakfasting with General Dessaix one morning, a man came in who followed the occupation of slave-merchant, and, after having saluted the French officer (seeing me in a different uniform) he requested to know who I was. Being told that I was an Englishman, he immediately came to me and began a conversation which I could not understand, but I could distinguish clearly the name of Haquin Bruce. I requested that the interpreter should be allowed to explain to me the merchant's meaning. I found he had been a guide with Mr. Bruce, in Abyssinia, and appeared very anxious to know if he was well, and ever intended to return, as he had promised.

'On the 16th, I started with a convoy for Suez, and arrived there on the 18th; when immediately preparations were made by General Boyer for my embarkation in a vessel, which he, by orders of General Kleber, gave me. She had been seized from an Arab merchant, and converted into a gun-boat, and rigged as a lugger.

'On the 19th, we sailed for Jedda with a crew of seven Arabs, a Chinese servant, whom I had hired at Cairo, and who had been a valet of Bonaparte's, but left there by him when he quitted Egypt – a French sailor, who concealed himself in the vessel, and an Arab girl given me by General Boyer; no arms, except a pair of pistols, and a sabre of my own. At this time the sea of Acaba swarmed with pirates, and it was only by putting a good face on the matter I escaped being taken; for the third day after leaving Suez, off Cape Raez Mahomed, we perceived, at daylight, two large dhows in chase of us. There was no time to deliberate; I immediately hauled in towards the largest, who, supposing me a French gunboat, made sail from me, leaving me at liberty to prosecute my voyage down the Red Sea.'

The Battle of St. Vincent
FEBRUARY 14, 1797 – VALENTINE'S DAY

'Sailor, on the darkening sea,
Lift the heart, and bend the knee!'

HEMANS

His Majesty's ship *Barfleur*, of ninety-eight guns, bearing the flag of Vice-Admiral Waldegrave, in the middle of the year 1795, sailed from Spithead to reinforce the fleet of Sir John Jervis, then blockading the French fleet in Toulon, and afterwards anchored in Gibraltar Bay. To speak of my sufferings from that nauseous disease, sea-sickness, in the Bay of Biscay, would probably excite no more commiseration in my readers, than they did from my more experienced messmates, who derided them, and comforted me with the idea of fat pork and pease-pudding, nautically called dog's body. I can only say, to me they were inexpressibly severe; and when my feet pressed *terra firma* at the ragged staff, Gibraltar, I thought myself in heaven. Oh, how I relished the firm-set earth, and the soft tack, and fresh butter it produced. But human felicity is of short duration; and a few hours again saw me pale, homesick, and miserable; and in course of time we joined the Mediterranean fleet, and, with tack and half-tack, took the bearings of Cape Sicia at noon, every day for nine months, diversified at times by putting into St. Fiorenza Bay in Corsica, for water and fresh beef. In the beginning of the year 1797, the *Fox* cutter came into the fleet, with the signal flying of having despatches of great importance to communicate to the commander-in-chief, who immediately hove-to, with a general signal for lieutenants. This *Fox* was noted for her quick passages, but more for her commander, Lieutenant Gibson, who was truly a fine specimen of the old English seamen, without having contracted their vulgarity. I have often met him at Admiral Waldegrave's table, for he was a universal favourite. In that skirmish of Lord Hotham's, not particularly flattering to our naval prowess, Gibson, in the little *Fox*, ran under the stern of the

Ça Ira, an eighty-gun ship, and loudly called on him to haul down
his colours, or he would sink him. The Frenchman smiled with
contempt, and the *Fox* broke all his stern windows with his six-
pounders. Alas, poor Gibson! This gallant officr fell a victim to the
rash attack made by Sir Horatio Nelson on Teneriffe. A heavy shot
from the batteries, pierced this beautiful and fragile fabric under
water, and she sunk with ninety seamen and marines, few of
whom were saved. One, of the fortunate few, I afterwards messed
with, and he used to electrify us with an account of his miraculous
escape – the way he shook off the clutch of the drowning wretches
around. He was dragged down, and touched the bottom three
times, and at last was getting into the dreamy state, which
concludes the dreadful sense of suffocation, he had before experienced, when a boat providentially saved him at the last gasp, to
adorn the navy, I believe, even to this day. But we have left the
Victory, Sir John Jervis, with the general signal for lieutenants.
This was speedily annulled, and substituted by the one for admi-
rals and captains to repair on board the commander-in-chief; this
made us aware the intelligence was of immense importance, and
made a great stir among the bigwigs. As I afterwards heard it
explained, Lady Hamilton, during the siesta of the King of Naples,
purloined a letter from his pocket, which he had been observed to
read with great agitation before dinner. The letter announced the
King of Spain's intention to join the coalition against England, and
invited his brother, Ferdinand of Naples, to make the blow
stronger by joining him. Our sovereignty of the sea was never
more strongly menaced. The northern powers had coalesced
under the Emperor Paul, and England stood singly, against a
world in arms. Rear-Admiral Mann was detached, with five sail of
the line, to Cadiz, and the fleet dispersed to various places to extri-
cate the British commerce; a few of the three-deckers accompanied
the commander-in-chief into St. Fiorenza Bay in Corsica, the
rendezvous of the Smyrna trade. The French fleet were on the
alert, and poured their troops into the island of Corsica, where we
were obliged to fight for our water; and many times have I seen
the gallant and skilful veteran, Sir J. Jervis, scrambling up the
rocks with all the alacrity of youth. At last, with ten sail of the line,
and each ship of war with a heavy merchantman in tow, we sailed
from St. Fiorenza Bay, closely followed by the Toulon fleet; so

closely, that no lights were displayed, nor guns allowed to be fired. After passing the straits of Gibraltar, His Majesty's sloop *Bonne Citoyenne*, joined the fleet, with intelligence that the Spaniards were at sea, under Don Cordova, to the immense number of twenty-seven sail of the line, and that of the largest size, accompanied by ten frigates, while rumours of the most portentous nature, stated their intention of proceeding to Brest, accompanied by the Toulon fleet; and by the junction of the grand French fleet, there awaiting them, to enter the British Channel above a hundred sail of the line, and to sweep it to the mouth of the Thames. Sir John Jervis, by the junction of Sir W. Parker, with five sail of the line, now numbered fifteen, and two frigates; and with this small comparative force he had to keep in check the Spanish Don, and show a bold front to the Toulon fleet, close on his heels, and outnumbering him. Never since England displayed her banner to the breeze, hath a British admiral been called upon for a decision on which the fate of his country more hung. If defeated in fight, Portugal must fall, and very few of his fleet would reach a British port. Pressed, on all sides, by a powerful and haughty enemy, with the northern powers on the alert, a defeat would be fatal to the interests, probably to the independence, of his country; and a further retreat into the Channel would be such a glaring confession of weakness, as probably to realise the fable of the sick lion, and bring all the minor states to kick at him in his helpless state. Sir John decided, like a brave man, to fight, and leave the event to Infinite Wisdom, in whose hands is the fate of nations; and I will bear testimony to the excellent discipline in which Sir John kept his fleet. It was a pattern to all others, and might, in some measure, have influenced his determination. At all events, on the 10th of February, the signal to clear for action announced the commander-in-chief's intention to fight against all odds, and in this he followed the advice that Lord Nelson always gave his captains in cases of doubt. His lordship used to say, 'Fight, and that closely, and you will not be thought very wrong.' I remember the care used in taking down the admiral's bulkheads, and the removal of all the furniture he could do without, below. The substitution of canvas, and the open, clear appearance of the long line of guns, which now were more frequently exercised, all assumed a more martial appearance, and the round, laughing, unintellectual countenance assumed a sharpened and eager look. On the 13th, *La Minerve*,[1] bearing the broad pendant of Commodore Sir Horatio Nelson, came down the Mediterranean, and joined the fleet. He was offered any ship of the line not bearing a flag, and with his characteristic modesty chose the smallest seventy-four – viz., the *Captain*. His pendant was flying on board of her a few hours after joining, and every heart warmed to see so brave and fortunate a warrior among us.

The 13th of February 1797, was employed by the British squadron, under Sir John Jervis, in getting ready for the ensuing fight, on which depended not only the fate of England, but the civilised world; for revolutionary jargon and demoralising principles spread like a baneful cloud over it, and went far to sap the first principles of social life, and restore the anarchy and confusion of the dark ages, when the strong hand alone gave law, and order was banished from among mankind. Grinding cutlasses, sharpening pikes, flinting pistols, among the boarders; filling powder, and fitting well-oiled gunlocks on our immense artillery by the gunners, slinging our lower yards with chains; and, in short, preparing a well-organised first-rate for this most important battle. The men and officers seemed to me to look taller, and the anticipation of victory was legibly written on each brow. It was my good fortune at that period to be in great favour with the vice-admiral; so much so, that each day he personally took me to where the grapes clustered his cabin, and the oranges in nettings hung thick above my head, with strong injunctions only to eat what had begun to decay. I was then, not quite thirteen, and strictly obeyed orders, *while he was in sight to enforce them*, otherwise a tempting peach, with its soft maiden blush, or the coarser red of juicy nectarine, diverted me from the straight and narrow path – I am sorry to reflect how frequently. The admiral, was a polished, good-natured gentleman, and always took me as midshipman of his boat, when mustering the crews of the ships of squadron in rotation. We one morning went on board the *Excellent*, Captain Cuthbert Collingwood, not then so cele-

[1] Commanded by that gallant officer, Sir George Cockburn, whose discipline and activity were the admiration of the fleet, and often induced Sir John Jervis to treat his friends by signalising the *Minerve* to chase. The way in which she spread her canvas seemed magical.

brated as he afterwards became, and I, being tired of seeing John Marlingspike and Tom Rattling smoothe down his front hair, and hitch up his trousers, preparatory to scraping his foot, with his best sea jerk, as he passed in review before the big-wigs, and pressed to go down by a brother mid, who felt proud of feasting the vice-admiral's aide-de-camp – and having internal conviction, as well as external, that the hour of noon had passed – the usual hour of dinner for young gentlemen – I, forgetting my proud station, stole from the vice-admiral's side, and was well employed in stowing my hold in the most expeditious manner with beef and pudding in the middy's berth, when all at once I heard, 'Pass the word for the vice-admiral's midshipman; his admiral and captain are towing alongside, waiting for him.' This alarming information nearly caused me to choke, by endeavouring to swallow a large piece of pudding I had in my mouth, and with my cocked hat placed on my head the wrong way, I crossed the hawse of Captain Collingwood, who, calling me a young scamp, and some other hard names, which I have long since forgiven, assured me, in not a very friendly tone, that if I was his midshipman, he would treat me with a dozen by marrying me to the gunner's daughter. This did not restore my self-possession; for, being rather of an imaginative turn, I had a slight suspicion that Captain Dacres[2] would very probably execute what his brother captain had hinted. But oh, the storm when I opened the gangway! a typhoon or hurricane must have appeared a calm compared to it; and in my hurry to jump into the boat, the *Excellent* having steerage way, I alighted on my captain's old-fashioned cocked hat. He seemed paralysed with rage; and the vice-admiral, who had not before spoken, with a quite smile told me to sit down, and asked me, in a kind voice, 'if my hunger was too great for his dinner?' I hung my head, like most culprits, and listened in silence to the captain's promised retribution; but I had a strong friend in the admiral, and was let off with a lecture as long as the main-top-bowline. During the long night of the 13th of February, we heard many heavy guns to wind-ward, and felt perfectly certain that they proceeded from the Spanish fleet, which could not be very remote. The day dawned in the east, and 'Up all hammocks,

[2] Afterwards Vice-Admiral James Richard Dacres, Commander-in-Chief at Jamaica. He died January 1810.

ahoy!' resounded through the decks of His Majesty's ship
Barfleur. Some were sent aloft to barricade the tops, while the
remainder were stowed with unusual care as a bulwark round the
upper decks. Great haze had prevailed during the night, and it
still continued. General signal flying on board the *Victory* for the
fleet to make all sail on the starboard tack, preserving a close
order of sailing in two lines, a vice-admiral leading each line, with
Sir John in the *Victory* two points on the weather-bow, our two
frigates and *La Bonne Citoyenne* sloop, under a press of sail, to
windward. At nine, the latter made the signal for a strange fleet to
windward; – then, that they were twenty-seven ships of the line
and ten frigates, with a cloud of small craft, and that they were
the Spanish fleet, under Don Cordova. These intimations of
approaching battle were received by the British squadron with
reiterated cheers; and so beautifully close was our order of sailing,
that the flying jib-boom of the ship astern projected over the
taffrail of her leader. Signal was made for the *Culloden* to chase to
windward, and after a short period, to form the line of battle,
without regard to the established order, by which manœuvre
Captain Troubridge led the British line; and one more competent
could not have been selected. Here we must admire that wonderful tact, and knowledge of human nature, possessed by Sir John
Jervis. Naval etiquette has established the senior captain as better
fitted to lead, from his experience, and he is so placed in the established order of battle; but practice has sometimes proved the
fallacy of such a theory; and Sir John, without offending, placed at
the head of his line, one of the most perfect seamen, though, as his
subsequent end proved, too daring, even to rashness. This ill-
fated officer took the *Culloden* home from Malta, when she had
been declared not seaworthy, and tried the same in the *Blenheim*
from India, and has never since been heard of; no doubt he fell a
victim to his rash daring. But on the 14th of February, no man
could have led the British line better, or better have proved the
unrivalled judgment of Sir John Jervis.

'I have a glimpse through the fog of their leeward line,' called
Signal-Lieutenant Edghill, from the mainyard, 'and they loom like
Beachy Head in a fog. By my soul, they are thumpers, for I
distinctly make out *four* tier of ports in one of them, bearing an
admiral's flag.'

'Don Cordova, in the *Santissima Trinidad*,' said the vice-admiral; 'and I trust in Providence that we shall reduce this mountain into a mole hill before sunset.'

The British had formed one of the most beautiful and close lines ever beheld. The fog drew up like a curtain, and disclosed the grandest sight I ever witnessed. The Spanish fleet, close on our weather bow, were making the most awkward attempts to form their line of battle, and they looked a complete forest huddled together; their commander-in-chief, covered with signals, and running free on his leeward line, using his utmost endeavours to get them into order; but they seemed confusion worse confounded. I was certainly very young, but felt so elated as to walk on my toes, by way of appearing taller, as I bore oranges to the admiral and captain, selecting some for myself, which I stored in a snug corner in the stern-galley, as a *corps de reserve*. The breeze was just sufficient to cause all the sails to sleep, and we were close hauled on the starboard tack, with royals set, heading up for the Spanish fleet. Our supporting ship, in the well-formed line, happened to be the *Captain*, and Captain Dacres hailed to say that he was desired by the vice-admiral to express his pleasure at being supported by Sir Horatio Nelson.

It wanted some time of noon when the *Culloden* opened her fire on the Spanish van, and our gallant fifteen, so close together, soon imitated her example. The roar was like heavy thunder, and the ship reeled and shook as if she was inclined to fall in pieces. I felt a choking sensation from the smell and smoke of gunpowder, and did serious execution on the oranges. This uproar and blinding appeared to me to have lasted a considerable time; but I judged more from my feelings than my watch, when I heard our active signal-lieutenant report the *Culloden's* signal to tack and break through the enemy's line, and the fleet to follow in succession. Down went the *Culloden's* helm, and she dashed through, as reported, for my vision was dazzled, between the nineteenth and twentieth ship of the enemy, closely followed by the *Colossus*, whose foreyard was shot away in the slings, as she was in stays.

'The *Captain* has put her helm down,' called the signal-luff.

'Only in the wind,' said the vice-admiral; 'she will box off directly.'

The admiral was wrong, and Commodore Sir Horatio Nelson went clean about, and dashed in among the Spanish van, totally unsupported, leaving a break in the British line – conduct totally unprecedented, and only to be justified by the most complete success with which it was crowned. After losing sight for some time of the little *Captain* among the leviathans of Spain, one of them, by some chance, appeared close under our stern; just as I had applied one of my select store of oranges to my mouth, she opened an ill-directed fire, apparently into the admiral's stern-galley, that I was viewing her from. The first bang caused a cessation of my labours, the second made me drop a remarkably fine Maltese orange, which rolled away and was no more seen, and the third made me close my commanders on the quarter-deck, bearing to each an orange. An opening in the Spanish forest now showed the *Captain* on board of two Spanish ships, large enough to hoist her in, and to our astonishment and joy, a tattered Union Jack fluttered above their sweeping ensigns. The commodore had made a bridge of one, to capture the other, and both were prizes to the *Captain*, Sir Horatio Nelson.

At this time, the fleets being much intermingled, Sir John bore up in the *Victory* to rake the *Salvador del Mundo*, who carried a rear-admiral's flag, and had been roughly used by the *Excellent*, which had passed on to assist the *Orion*, engaged by the *Santissima Trinidad*. What a smashing broadside was sent into the unfortunate Spaniard's stern by the *Victory!* and before she could digest such a dose, we delivered another, which caused the Spanish flag to be quickly lowered, leaving our following friend to take possession of her.

When the British squadron passed through the Spanish fleet, they cut out eight ships of the line, who then tacked, and kept hovering to windward of their distressed friends. The rear division now perceived the imminent peril of their commander-in-chief, who was dismasted and very hard pressed; indeed, it was roundly asserted that he struck his colours, and re-hoisted them on the rear division bearing down to his succour. The *Conde Reigle*, who led this division, ranging up alongside of His Majesty's ship *Britannia*, received one of the most destructive broadsides, and hauled her wind in a great hurry, taking no further part in the action.

The time now nearly five p.m., and two first-rates and two second-rates showed the gay Union of England fluttering over the ensign of Spain. Our prizes and disabled ships had fallen to leeward, and as the day was closing, Sir John, who must have been amazed at his own success, made the signal for the fleet to re-form the line of battle to leeward, and bore up in the *Victory* to close them, and formed his line just to windward of his prizes, between them and the Spanish fleet, which still remained in the greatest disorder, their commander-in-chief, in the *Santissima*, with only her mainmast and mainyard standing. I believe the slaughter on board her so unprecedented, that Don Cordova, on shifting his flag, stated he had left four hundred of his men dead on her decks. The captured ships had suffered much, and certainly took a glutton's share of beating with apathetic composure, their return being very feeble. Had the daring and heroic soul of Nelson been infused into the breast of every British commander on that glorious day, every one of their gorgeous ensigns would have bowed to the Jack of England, and Sir John Jervis would have been created a duke, instead of Earl St. Vincent.

Our fleet, during the night, which was fine, repaired damages and shifted prisoners, both fleets lying to, with a prospect of renewing the fight at daylight. At dawn of day, the Spaniards, exasperated at their unexpected defeat and heavy losses, made a demonstration of fight, by forming the line of battle, and placing their heads towards us, bringing up with them a very light breeze. An affirmative to the question, 'Are you ready to renew the action?' flew at the masthead of each of our ships of the line, as the leeward ones, mostly disabled, were towed into the British line of battle. At this moment a violent explosion from our lower-deck, with the hasty flight of the port, part of the side, and a round shot of thirty-two pounds, through the air, caused great excitement; and the cry of fire ensuing, caused some confusion in the *Barfleur*. This was speedily got under, and our captain made his appearance on the quarter-deck completely drenched, and proceeded to inquire into the late alarming occurrence. The men had slept at quarters, and one of them was soundly sleeping on the breech of a lower-deck gun, that was housed. A waister from the sister-kingdom, rather raw in the service, possessed of an inquiring mind, was at a loss to determine how pulling a string affixed to the lock could cause such a thundering noise; in his philosophical experiment he had placed the lock on full cock, gave a gentle pull with the aforesaid string, fired the gun, killed the sleeper, smashed his foot to pieces by the recoil, and stood transfixed with horror and pain at the success of his experiment. The loss of his foot saved his back, and the carpenters soon repaired the damage. Whether the noise of our shot was the cause, or that the better part of valour influenced the Dons, they hauled their wind, which now began to freshen, and increased their distance. By signal from the commander-in-chief, the British fleet hoisted Spanish colours, in compliment to Don something[3] – whose flag had been flying on board the *Salvador del Mundo*, and who was now dying of wounds received in the action. Whether this refined compliment cheered his moments of agony, I cannot say, but it received its reward by a rich Spanish ship running into the midst of us, being bothered by both fleets appearing with the same colours.

Sir John, satisfied with the honour he had gained, and entertaining a well-founded dread of the Toulon fleet, which he would have found a very rough customer, shaped a course for Lagos Bay, on the coast of Portugal, with the prizes in tow; the Spanish fleet following us, though evidently afraid to come within gunshot.

On the following morning we anchored in battle order across this open bay, and in the evening a gale of wind came in from the sea, and the fleet was in terrible jeopardy, most of the ships with their sheet anchor down, and some with their spare one. In the *Barfleur* we were pitching bows under, with three anchors ahead; one mile astern of us extended a reef of rocks, on which the sea broke frightfully, and through which there appeared no opening; half a mile within them lay a populous village of fishermen, and as they expected a God-send by the wreck of the whole fleet, they had gone through the trouble of collecting wood and burning fires through the night. Young as I was, I retain a strong recollection of this dark and dreadful night.

'Ship ahead driving,' called the forecastle lieutenant.

'God help us!' I heard the captain piously ejaculate. 'Lower-deck there, stand by, to veer on the three cables at the same time – place the helm hard a starboard' – and the commander-in-chief, in his gallant and noble ship, the *Victory*, passed our starboard side close, driving fast upon the rocks to leeward, which shook off the heavy sea, throwing its white spray to the clouds. There was an

[3] Don Francisco Xavier Winthuysen, Rear-Admiral, who died of his wounds received on board the *San Joseph*. His sword was presented by Nelson to the city of Norwich.

agonised cry of horror, and 'O God! save her!' as this beautiful fabric hastened on destruction. We heard her last effort, as her spare anchor flashed in the briny flood, and, thank God, she brought up with four anchors a-head. Never shall I forget the sight, as I caused our stern and top lanterns to be relighted. The roaring of the wind and rain, the bellowing noise of the officers' trumpets, the booming of the numerous guns of distress, the roar of the breakers so near us astern, and the ghastly reflection of the surf and fires ashore – all, all are imprinted on my memory, to the year in which I write.

Recollections of Tom Allen.
the Last of the Agamemnons

The monuments and memorials of the immortal Nelson are widely scattered over the kingdom, to die only when the name of British valour shall be forgotten, but the living witnesses and partners of his glory are rapidly passing from amongst us. One of the most interesting, though least conspicuous of the few that long survived their leader, was his faithful body-servant, Tom Allen, who, at last, was struck by the hand of death with almost as much celerity as if he had fallen on the deck of the *Victory*.

This fine specimen of the true British tar was born at Burnham Thorpe, in the county of Norfolk, in the year 1764, and, from his earliest years, had been in the service of the Nelson family. He had always exhibited a warm attachment to the person of the great Nelson, and it was to this strong feeling, rather than to a distinct love of fame, we must attribute Tom's having consented to resign his home on *terra firma*, for the perilous life of a sailor. When Nelson was appointed to the *Agamemnon*, Tom consented to follow his young master's fortunes, being then just nineteen years of age. A raw country lad, labouring under the inconvenience of a violent Norfolk dialect, which he never lost, he was not looked upon as an interesting or important addition to the captain's suite; but the salt water soon gave him a polish, and his faithful services did not long remain unnoticed, or fail in obtaining for him the respect due to fidelity. In due time, Tom became more and more useful to his master, and at length, being almost necessary,[1] was considered his most trusty servant; in fact, he was for a time looked upon as a part and parcel of his master, and, on shore or on board, was a constant appendage. Tom had the custody of Captain Nelson's plate, jewels, everything, even his person, was in some measure in Tom's custody, for on all visits ashore, or when ill from wounds, he slept near his master; and when from the latter cause, as was sometimes the case,

[1] Next to Lady Hamilton, Tom Allen possessed the greatest influence with his heroic master.'

his master had not the strength of voice to awaken his *wally de sham*, a string was affixed to Tom's shirt collar for that purpose. As a matter of course, Tom accompanied the great hero in the *Captain*, the *Minerve* (Captain Cockburne),[2] in which the commodore had hoisted his broad pendant *protempore*, and the *Theseus*, successively, until the untoward event at Teneriffe. It was not his good fortune to have been on shore on that occasion, but he was present at the amputation of the hero's arm, an event he was in the habit of describing with much feeling. Tom's service was nearly equal in length to that of his captain; he had shared in those numerous perils and triumphs, that render Nelson's career the most glorious epoch of our naval history, and the regard of his master seemed to acquire strength by the addition of each year to the acquaintance. Formally installed into the office of confidential man, he returned, as a matter of course, with his master to England, in the *Seahorse*; and when the gallant commodore was restored to a more robust health, Tom accompanied him to the Mediterranean. He was in attendance on his master during that anxious and persevering chase of the French fleet, which ended so gloriously for England and for Nelson, in the destruction of that powerful armament in Aboukir Bay. The glory of this day, the brightest in the whole of Tom Allen's useful and honest life, the brave fellow was in the constant practice of describing, upon every possible opportunity; and between his irregularity of manner and dialect, and the inordinate degree of vanity under which he evidently laboured in the recital, he succeeded in exciting in his hearers a highly favourable opinion of his loyalty, courage, and kind-heartedness. With the victory of the Nile, Tom's character as a hero terminated; and although he accompanied the admiral in the attack on Copenhagen, on board the *Elephant*, he did not appear to glory in the doings of that day, and never spoke of them unless pressed to do so. In action, Tom was generally stationed at one of the upper-deck guns, and became, in time, as well used to fighting as it was necessary Nelson's follower should be. Although from certain little observations in which he had been known to indulge, it is evident that the proverb, 'No man is a hero to his *valet de chambre*,' was in some degree exemplified in this instance also; yet it was impossible that anyone could be about Nelson without being inspired with esteem and

[2] Vide *Memoir of Rear-Admiral Sir Thomas M. Hardy*, vol. iii. p. 254, *et seq*.

reverence, as was in reality the case with Tom Allen. Speaking of the celebrated action of the fourteenth of February, Tom delighted to detail the deeds of his master; nor would he, when closely pressed, deny that he fought at his side[3] when boarding the *San Nicholas*. In his narrative of the battle of Aboukir, Tom never forgot to mention that it was the admiral's intention to have dressed himself in full uniform previous to going into action; but that, with the freedom of a sailor, and the influence he was then able to exercise over him, he induced his master to forego his intention. As the battle of the Nile was a night action, the particular dress of the admiral could not have been a point of importance, but Tom was under the impression, and he did not become less obstinate as his years increased, that it was in consequence of the dress worn by Lord Nelson at Trafalgar, that he lost his life: this assertion was the uniform preface to another opinion, to which he tenaciously adhered during his life, viz.: 'that had he, Tom Allen, been Lord Nelson's *wally de sham* at that time, he would have prevented his master from putting on the coat he wore, and therefore, that he would not have fallen in the battle of Trafalgar.' Tom's logic is a little deficient, it wants that *vis consequentiæ*, so valuable to just reasoning, as our hero might have been killed on that memorable day, in whatever dress Tom might have proposed; besides, it has been clearly shown that it was a chance bullet, and not one especially aimed at Nelson, which gave him his death-wound. The smoke which obscured every object at the distance of fifteen or sixteen yards, it may reasonably be supposed, precluded the possibility of any man's selecting Nelson in particular; and therefore, we may fairly conjecture, that poor Tom's excellent intention, even had he succeeded in it, would have been frustrated by the hand of Providence, who ordained the most glorious death for his master, and the one which, if he had been allowed a choice, he would to a certainty have fixed on. He fell in the consummation of a victory the greatest in its consequences, and most decisive in itself, upon record.

It is supposed that Tom partook of some of the weakness of our nature, and from too much indulgence became too useful: as this

[3] 'When under fire from the ports of Valetta, which hulled the ship, and knocked away our fore-topmast, this faithful servant interposed his bulky form between those forts and his little master.'

was not an error of the heart, having had his judgment corrected by a brief suspension from the duties, but not the emoluments of his office, he was again reinstated in his original powers, and domiciled at Merton. In the year 1837, some of those jewels, of which Tom had once the care, were discovered in the Town Hall of Southwark, and the rumour reaching Greenwich Hospital, Sir Thomas Hardy directed Tom Allen to wait upon the magistrates, and identify the different articles. The appearance of the brave tar, then in his seventy-third year, excited considerable interest, which was much heightened by the account he gave of his services while *wally de sham* to Admiral Nelson.[4]

When Nelson took leave of his home at Merton, and joined the fleet destined for Cadiz, in September 1805, Tom Allen's services being required on shore for some time after his master's departure, the *Victory* sailed without him. He had received orders to follow, and join the ship as soon as possible, but the poor fellow had exceeded the time limited for sailing, and the last ship had quitted Portsmouth before his arrival there. This misfortune pressed heavily on the hardy sailor for the remainder of his life: the battle of Trafalgar had been fought, Nelson, even in death, victorious, and, in these tremendous scenes, the story of which will be told after ages shall have rolled by, Tom might have been an actor, had he only reached Portsmouth in time for the last ship of the fleet.

When Nelson descended into the tomb, many of the brave fellows who had shared his dangers, but not his glory, were thrown on the resources of their own manly minds. Returning home to Burnham Thorpe, Tom sought the means of sustaining his wife and family by such occupations and services as a rural district affords. There, his sheet-anchor was Captain Sir W. Bolton, R.N., of Coltesey, Norwich, in whose service he continued until the decease of that benevolent individual, after which, Tom was once more sent adrift. His situation from this point became rapidly more distressing; his age, the peculiar habits of his former life, the broken-hearted feelings of a man who was the favourite follower, the confidential servant of the most illustrious of England's naval heroes, all these circumstances tended to unfit him for any

---

[4] The circumstances of this singular discovery, as well as a particular account of Tom's visit to Southwark Town Hall, will be found in Clarke and M'Arthur's *Life of Nelson*, vol. ii. p. 138.

occupation, and to embitter his declining years. The workhouse was the only coast in view, and there, every day, he expected to be thrown. It was at this critical moment in his earthly cruise, that a friendly sail hove in sight; kind Providence now conducted a benevolent and patriotic individual,[5] to the sailor's cottage, who gave him that protection which his country, probably, should have anticipated. But this generous man was the instrument through which the blessings of God were, in this instance, to be distributed, and the persevering zeal with which he put forward poor Tom's just claims upon his country, cannot be sufficiently applauded, or his generous example too conspicuously exhibited to society. Remembering that Sir Thos. Hardy, then one of the Lords of the Admiralty, had been Nelson's friend, and also his flag-captain for several years, in which situation he must frequently have witnessed the officious zeal of Tom for his master's happiness, Mr. Scott submitted the poor fellow's case to his humane consideration, and solicited his co-operation in placing the old sailor in a situation of comfort and independence, to which his services had fairly entitled him.

A second coadjutor, with whose name and character the reader of Nelson's life is necessarily familiar, was found by Mr. Scott, in Sir W. Beatty, M.D., formerly surgeon on board the *Victory*, but at this period physician to the Royal Hospital at Greenwich.[6] With the assistance of these influential individuals, Mr. Scott succeeded in obtaining a berth for his honest protégé in that noble asylum, into which he was, at length, admitted a pensioner in the year 1831. The first round of the ladder being gained, the second would have been ascended with less difficulty, had Tom enjoyed the blessings of a moderate education in his youth; but being totally illiterate, he was ineligible for promotion in the public service. This unfortunate check to his ambition being communicated to Sir Jahleel Brenton, Bart, lieutenant-governor of the Hospital, he immediately employed Tom in the capacity of gardener. In this new sphere of action, his indefatigable industry was found to compensate for the absence of horticultural skill; and his scrupulous integrity gained him the confidence of the lieutenant-governor. Beyond the duties

[5] P. N. Scott, Esq., of Norwich, a gentleman of independent fortune, who had formerly been a surgeon in the royal navy.

[6] Vide *Life and Services of Admiral Lord Nelson*, vol. iii. p. 157.

of his ostensible occupation, his quiet and temperate habits and uninterrupted cheerfulness rendered him in every way trustworthy. The emoluments of his little stewardship, and an occasional lift from his old shipmates, enabled him to rub along, and keep his old wife and their granddaughter tolerably comfortable; while his excellent qualities secured for him the respect of the heads of the institution in which he was sheltered. Rear-Admiral Sir Thomas Hardy having been appointed governor of Greenwich Hospital, Tom's star was at once in the ascendant, and, on the 18th of June 1837, the consummation so devoutly to be wished for, at length took place, in the appointment of Lord Nelson's old servant to the office of 'Pewterer' to the Hospital. For Tom, this was no mean service, being accompanied by a salary of sixty-five pounds per annum, with apartments in the west hall of the Hospital, and there his wife and his granddaughter continued to share with him those rewards of his humble, but not inglorious life, until Tom set out for 'that undiscovered country, from whose bourne no traveller returns.'

Greenwich Hospital might have furnished forth many nobler wrecks of the British veteran than Tom personally presented, but there never was a more thorough sailor, in thought, feeling, and action.

This genuine original, is said to have supplied the anecdotes of Captain Chamier's 'Ben Brace,' and he was known to have betrayed indignation, when he understood that he had made his appearance in the world under any name but his own. Allen always reminded his visitors of one of the shattered masts of his former dwelling; his face was seared by wind and weather, but there was an unyielding strength about his stunted frame, that seemed to defy the attacks of time: his long hair was almost as black, and his eye as piercing, as when he was in his youth, and might, according to his own belief, 'have married either of the princesses of Naples, had he been so minded.' He was a mixture of honest hardihood, untutored simplicity, pardonable vanity, and nautical prejudice; a fine example of the British tar, who acknowledges but three principles of action – love for his country, hatred for his enemies, and veneration for his captain. And of that country Tom deserved well, for, beside being the faithful servant, or, as he styled himself, '*the wally de sham*,' of her noblest hero, he wore away the vigour of his arm in her defence (to use his own phraseology) '*in fourteen skrimmages and fifteen reg'lar engagements,*' not to mention 'affairs' of inferior note, being wounded three several times, once most severely; but, as he often ejaculated, 'thanks be to God, his precious eyes and limbs were spared!'

Tom's yarn was now, at the close of 1838, nearly spun out, although none observed its slender quality; and on the 23rd day of November in that year, 'the last of the Agamemnons' expired without a groan, in that grand temple of English gratitude, where he had for a few previous years resided. The truly benevolent heart needs no other compensation than the sense of its own rectitude; but justice, generosity, and the force of example, demand the warmest acknowledgments to the individual who had espoused honest Tom's cause, and so unremittingly persevered in placing him in a position honourable alike to himself and his country. The benevolent conduct of Mr. Scott, in inspiring those that possessed the power, with the inclination likewise, to save the brave veteran, has been most cordially acknowledged by the respectable instruments of the poor fellow's promotion, and their prompt contribution to his happiness as life declined; and one of his kindest friends, patrons, and benefactors, after his admission to the Hospital, Sir Jahleel Brenton, thus communicated the circumstances of his death to his old patron, on the day next after his decease, as a just tribute to that gentleman's benevolent and exemplary conduct.

'Greenwich Hospital, 24th November 1838. – My Dear Sir, – It is with deep regret that I inform you that poor old Tom Allen is no more. He was taken off most suddenly and most unexpectedly last night. He was apparently in the enjoyment of high health, and looking remarkably well, when we saw him only a few days before. His wife had gone to town yesterday, and poor Allen had been walking before the coach-office, expecting the arrival of the omnibus in the evening, when it is supposed he got thoroughly chilled, for, at the time of his wife's arrival, she found him seized with spasms, and he was immediately taken to the infirmary. The poor woman herself was so ill as to render it necessary that she should be conveyed to her apartments and put to bed, where she still remains, and in such a state that the medical attendants will not allow her to be informed of her husband's death. Lady Brenton has just been to see her, and is very much distressed at the state in which she found her: every care shall be taken of her, and I will not fail to communicate further respecting her. I very much regret having to make you acquainted with a circumstance which will give you so much pain, but you will have the comfort of reflecting that you have been the means of making the last years of poor Allen's life happy. Lady Brenton joins me in kindest regards and best wishes to Mrs. Scott and your daughter. Very sincerely yours – J. Brenton.'

This feeling communication, little less honourable to the writer than to his amiable correspondent, was soon after followed by a second from Rear-Admiral Sir T. Hardy, governor of the Hospital, from which we extract a few lines that tend to illustrate our 'story of a life.' 'Greenwich Hospital, 29th November, 1838. – Sir Thomas Hardy regrets, in common with Mr. Scott, the loss of poor Tom Allen, but was happy to have it in his power to contribute to his comfort in the latter days of his life.' The coldness of office, the distance of rank, may appear in the brief note of the governor, but his heart was as warm in that elevated position, as when he and Tom Allen had sailed together; and the record of his regard for his old shipmate, is preserved by a tablet which the governor caused to be erected over his grave, in the Hospital cemetery, bearing this inscription: 'To the memory of Thomas Allen, the faithful servant of Lord Nelson, born at Burnham Thorpe, in the county of Norfolk 1764, and died at the royal Hospital, Greenwich, on the 23rd of November 1838.' Thus, while the dome of St. Paul's forms a mausoleum of his noble master, worthy of his greatness, the servant in his death is not less gratefully remembered.

Tom was blessed with a family, and his eldest hope, 'a chip of the old block,' a strong athletic man, had long ceased to be a burden to his parents: selecting a rustic life, he became an honest labourer, at Fakenham, in his native county of Norfolk, and never lost any becoming opportunity of acknowledging 'that his name was Horatio, and that the great Lord Nelson was his godfather.'

The situation which Tom held in the Hospital did not entitle his widow to a pension, so that at his fall the active benevolence of Tom's fast friend in life, Mr. Scott, was again called into operation, in raising a subscription amongst his friends for the future provision of the poor widow. Whether every reminiscence of Nelson is called to mind with grateful sentiments in the hero's country, or whether warm admiration of Mr. Scott's humane exertions secured for his labours a cordial support, or, which is most probable, the combination of both causes operated, the subscription, which he suggested, received the most liberal patronage; and the benefactor of Tom Allen and his family enjoyed this comfortable reflection, that, having first given the nation an opportunity of rewarding one of her bravest veterans – one who occupied an interesting position in our fleet – he was again the means of rendering us his debtor, by taking care that we should not leave the widow of poor Tom to die neglected.

The activity of Mr. Scott in furthering the latter national object, for certainly Tom's widow was better entitled to a public pension than hundreds that we have known of in higher life, is fully, fairly, and faithfully related, and the rapid success of his amiable efforts, may be collected from the following communication from his friend and coadjutor, Lieutenant Rivers, R.N., with which we shall conclude our recollections of 'The Last of the Agamemnons' – an humble sequel to the memoirs of his great master.

'Greenwich Hospital, 3rd of April 1839. – My Dear Sir, – I have to acknowledge the receipt of your letter of the 1st instant. I communicated your wishes to Sir W. Beatty, who bid me thank you for the newspaper, and acquaint you, that Dr. Andrew B—d resides in Clarges Street, Piccadilly. I believe I have added all the names to my list. I this day added it up, and find it amounts to £106 18s. – *really you have done wonders* – say nothing about what you may reasonably expect. On the other side I have given you a summary of the subscription. I have not shown it to Sir Thomas lately – he will be surprised. I do hope to find Nelson's undertaker liberal, and that your returns from Malta will be equally so. There appears no bounds to your strenuous exertions. If you find your interview with Lord N—n free and conversant, you may tell him, Lieutenant Rivers, of Greenwich Hospital, who owes his appointment to the late Lord Nelson (prebendary of Canterbury), has a son passed nearly four years, with high testimonials of character, and cannot get him made a lieutenant. This may appear a hard case to one who was his lordship's aide-de-camp in the action, and received a slap in the face with a splinter, that knocked out two or three teeth, and shortly after he found himself minus a leg; but here is a living witness of God's mercy, and will, as long as he draws the breath of life, venerate the name of "Nelson."

'I went to R—'s rooms in Regent Street, to see the designs and models for the Nelson monument; few were good, and much rubbish amongst them: it appears the committee thought so too, and ordered them to try again. I find half a dozen more names will fill the front side of my subscription list. I shall feel delighted to fill the other side. You will have the goodness to remember me to the old widow, and believe me, my dear sir, yours very sincerely – W. Rivers.'

Index

Abbreviations

Adm = Admiral; Capt = Captain; Cdre = Commodore; Fr = French; Gen = General; Hon = Honourable; HMS = His Majesty's Ship; Lt = Lieutenant; R/A = Rear-Admiral; Sp = Spanish; V/A = Vice-Admiral

Abercrombie, Gen. Sir R 42
  at landings in Egypt 51–52
  death of 56–59
Aboukir Bay 137
  battle of (1798) 5, 9, 176
  landings at (1801) 50–53
Acton, Sir J 3, 29
Agamemnon, HMS 127, 175
Alexandria 50, 114, 140–141
Allen, Tom 5, 30, 127–132, 175–184
Almiraz, Gen. 157, 158, 159
Aruba 80

Ball, Capt 9
Barbadoes 122
Barfleur, HMS 123, 127, 134, 163, 168, 171, 172
Batavia, HMS 5
Beaver, Capt Philip 54, 56
Berry, Capt Sir Edward 33
  battle with *Guillaume Tell* 15–29
  pursuit of *Le Généreux* 7–9
Bickerton, Sir Richard 52
Blackwood, Capt. The Hon. 16, 17, 21, 28
Blenheim, HMS 168
Bonaparte, Gen. Napoleon 143, 151–152, 157, 158, 159, 160
Bonne Citoyenne, HM Sloop 165, 168

Britannia, HMS 170
Burnham Thorpe (Norfolk) 130, 175

Ça Ira (Fr) 164
Caledonian, HMS 73
Captain, HMS 166, 169–170, 175
Caraccioli, Adm. 1–5
Carthagena 59, 60
Centaur, HMS 142
Christian, Sir Hugh 150, 151
Cochrane, Capt. Hon. A 50
Coffield, Capt. 129
Collier, Capt. Sir George 68–71
Collingwood, Capt. Cuthbert 166, 167
Colossus, HMS 169
Conde Reigle (Sp) 170
Copenhagen, battle of (1801) 176
Cordova, Don 165, 168, 169, 171
Culloden, HMS 168, 169
Curaçoa 81–82
  attack on Fyke Fort 83–88
  blockade of 89–98
Culver, Billy 133–136

Dacres, V/A J R 18, 123–124, 167, 169
Dangereux, HM Gun Vessel 160
Decrés, R/A 15, 16, 17, 18, 23, 28, 103
Dessaix, Gen. 160–161
Dixon, Cdre Sir Manley 15, 16

Djezzar Pasha 45
Dordrecht, HMS 150
Duckworth, Adm Sir John 111
Dugauez Firman (Fr) 149
Dundas, Hon. L 38, 41

Egypt, British landings in *see* Aboukir
  Bay, landings at
El Arish, Convention of 160
El Carmen, HMS 114, 137, 138,
  142, 147
Elephant, HMS 176
Elk, HM Sloop 59
Erskine, Lt 38, 40
Excellent, HMS 166, 167, 170

Fleming, Lt J 83, 84, 99–101
Fort Amsterdam (Curaçoa) 96
Foudroyant, HMS 1, 3, 7, 9, 11, 41, 58,
  123, 127, 130, 147
  battle with *Guillaume Tell* 15–29
  fire aboard 53–56
  gale off Marmorice 43–44
  royal visit at Palermo to 24–27
  royal cruise 29–32
Fox, HM Cutter 163–164
Fyke Fort (Curaçoa) 81–82, 83–88, 99

Gibson, Lt 163–164
Go-Along, HM Brig 101–103
Greenwich Hospital 127, 130, 179
Guillaume Tell (Fr) 15–29, 31, 33, 148

Hamilton, Emma 1, 3, 4, 5, 11, 12,
  27, 28–29, 31, 32, 33–34, 35, 127,
  131, 164
  description of 6–7
  influence over Nelson 5–6, 23–24
Hamilton, Sir William 7, 12, 15,
  32–33, 35
Hardy, Capt 127–128, 130, 178, 179,
  180, 182
Hercule, HMS 113
Hispaniola 115

Hood, Lord 133

Inglis, Capt 43–44

Jamaica 89, 113
Janverin, Capt Richard 143, 147–148
  narrative of 149–161
Jervis, Sir J *see* St Vincent, Lord

Keith, Adm Lord 5, 35, 41, 42–43, 45,
  49, 50, 52, 54, 59, 150
Kléber, Gen 140, 159, 160, 161
  execution of his assassin 140–141
Knight, Miss Cornelia 7, 31
  poem for Lady Hamilton 31

La Fortuné, HMS 89, 90, 94, 100
La Franchise, HMS 82, 87, 89, 94, 98,
  99, 100, 101
La Minerve, HMS 166
La Rochelle 73
Le Généreux (Fr) 7, 8, 12
Leghorn (Livorno) 35, 37
Lion, HMS 15, 16
Little, Lt 73, 75, 76
L'Orient 68–69, 71

M'Donnel, Capt. Rundel ('Mad Mac')
  73–88, 99
Mack, Gen. 2
Maitland, Lt Edward 113–116
Malta 9, 15–16, 33–35, 130, 131
Mann, R/A 164
Marmorice Bay 42, 44–45
Menou, Gen 51, 53, 140
Merton (Surrey) 5–6
Mexico, Gulf of 59
Minorca, HMS 15
Minerve, HMS 176
Missiessy, R/A 111
Moore, Capt. Sir Graham 104
Murray, Capt The Hon. John 82, 83,
  89, 94–97, 99
Mustapha Bey 28

Naples 1–5, 130
Neale, Adm. Sir H Burrard 68, 73, 76
Nepean, Sir Evan 133–134
Neiza, Marquis de 128
Negress, HM Gun-vessel 156, 160
Nelson, Lord 1, 4, 5, 6, 11, 12, 15, 27, 34, 147–148, 160, 175, 176, 177
    battle of St Vincent 164–166, 169, 171
    chase of Le *Généreux* 8–9
    description of 7
    dinner aboard *Foudroyant* 29–30, 127–130
    orders and decorations 7
    receives Neapolitan royal family aboard *Foudroyant* 24–26
Nesbit, Capt 24
Northumberland, HMS 8, 9

Orient (Fr), wreck of 50
Orion, HMS 68–71, 170

Paget, Sir Arthur 35
Paget, Gen Sir E 144
Pakenham, Capt. Edmund 149, 150
Palermo 9, 10–13, 24–29, 160
Palermo, Prince of 13
    aboard *Foudroyant* 16, 20–21, 34
Parker, Sir William 165
Parsons, Lt George Samuel
    aboard *El Carmen* 137–148
    aboard sinking *Orion* 68–71
    and the rats 104–106
    and Lady Hamilton 5–6
    at ball at Palermo 9–13
    at pursuit of Le *Généreux* 7–9,
    at pursuit of *Guillaume Tell* 15–29
    attack on Fyke Fort, Curaçoa 83–88
    battle of St Vincent 163–173
    blockade of Curaçoa 89–98
    collision with Sir William Hamilton 33
    dinner with Nelson 30, 127

    fire aboard *Foudroyant* 53–56
    gale off Marmorice 42–45
    gunboat attack off Carthagena 59–65
    meets Billy Culver 134
    night attack on Point du Ché 73–77
    storming of the Dutch camp on Curaçoa 99–101
Peard, Capt. 8, 35
Pelican, HM Brig 102–103
Penelope, HMS 15, 17, 21, 23
Perrée, R/A 9
Petrel, HMS 43
Pique, HMS 114
Plymouth 71
Point Du Ché 73, 74
Port Mahon brig 16
Port Royal, Jamaica 110–111, 112, 122
'Port Royal Lion', the 110–111
Portsmouth 104, 116
Principio Real (Port) 33
Proby, Capt The Hon 57–58

Queen Charlotte, HMS 35
    destruction of 37–42

Racoon, HMS 79
Reindeer, HMS 94
Resistance, HMS 149, 150
    loss of 151
Rhodes 50
Rochefort 73
Royal William, HMS 106, 134, 135
Ruffo, Cardinal 1, 3, 4

Salvador del Mundo (Sp) 170, 172
San Nicholas (Sp) 177
Santissima Trinidad (Sp) 169, 170, 171
Selby, Capt William 114, 137, 138, 139, 141, 142, 144, 145, 146, 147
Smith, Sir Sidney 56, 137, 138, 141, 142, 143, 144, 145–146, 151–152, 156, 157, 158, 159, 160

description of 137, 144
diet of rats 144–145
St Domingo 107–109, 111
St Elmo, bombardment of 34
St Vincent, Adm Lord 6, 163–173
St Vincent, Battle of 18, 163–173
Success, HMS 8, 34
Theseus, HMS 156, 176

Thurn, Count 1
Tigre, HMS 143, 151, 152, 153, 156, 157, 158, 159

Todd, Capt
at destruction of *Queen Charlotte* 37, 38, 40
Troubridge, Capt. 168
Trench, Mrs Richard 6

Valiant, HMS 73
Vanguard, HMS 2
Vardo Bay 127–128
Victory, HMS 164, 168, 171, 172, 174, 178, 179

Waldegrave, V/A 18, 163

Also in the *Sailors' Tales* Series:
THE NARRATIVE
OF
WILLIAM SPAVENS
A Chatham Pensioner, by Himself

There are probably less than a dozen known copies of the original 1796 edition of this book in the whole of the UK, yet historians and writers of the calibre of Nicholas Rodger and Dudley Pope have regularly praised its intelligence and insight. It is particularly valuable in being a literate view from the ordinary seaman – itself unusual – but also in covering the pre-Nelsonic navy. Spavens, therefore, offers an alternative view to the usual top-down history, and has much to say on the emotive topic of press gangs, for example, and a stirring eyewitness account of Hawke's great victory in Quiberon Bay in 1759. Besides outlining his own fascinating career, Spavens also describes in great detail the ships, organisation and social life of the superb navy of Anson's day, as well as guiding the reader around many of the port-cities which he knew firsthand.

Spavens was born in Lincolnshire in 1734 and went to sea at an early age, being pressed out of merchantman into the Roayl Navy in time to fight in the Seven Years War. He was injured in an accident in 1764, which eventually resulted in the amputation of his lower leg thirty years later, the publication of his memoirs being an attempt to supplement the meagre pension provided by the Chatham Chest. His sea going career was only a decade, but in that time he visited North America, the West Indies, the Baltic, the Mediterranean, and the East Indies, and retained vivid memories of them all.

216 x 138mm, 192pp, £9.95 paperback
ISBN 186176 083 3

For an illustrated catalogue of all Chatham Publishing books, contact:
The Marketing Department, Chatham Publishing
61 Frith Street, London W1V 5TA
Tel: 0171 434 4242 Fax: 0171 434 4415